THE CARESS AND THE HURT

THE CARESS AND THE HURT

Prose and Verse
Clarine Coffin Grenfell

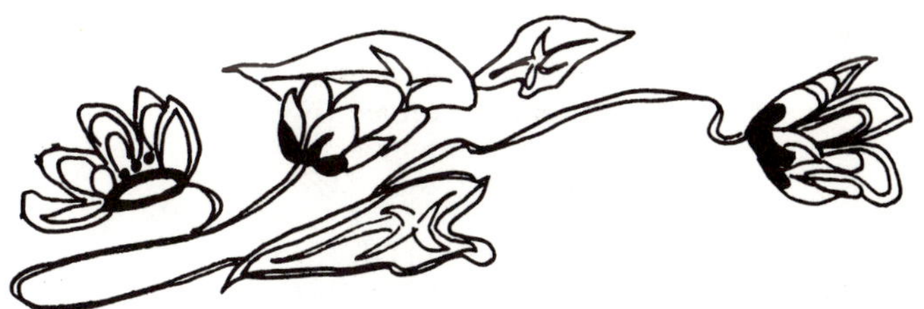

Line Drawings:
Lornagrace Grenfell Bowron

Other books by the same author:

Women My Husband Married

Roses in December

First printing, May, 1982
Second printing, January, 1983
Third printing, September, 1983
Fourth printing, June, 1984

**A Publication Of
GRENFELL READING CENTER
Alamoosook Lake
Orland, Maine 04472**

LIBRARY OF CONGRESS CATALOG NUMBER: 82-90161

ISBN: 0-9612766-0-6

PRINTED IN THE UNITED STATES OF AMERICA BY
LITHOGRAPHICS, INC., CANTON, CT 06019

. . . for Bart
who always says, "That's good, Suke."

. . . for Marjorie, John, Dorothy, Ken —
and all other encouragers

. . . and especially for Jack
whose love and faith never faltered

CONTENTS

OF THE SCHOOL

OF THE CHURCH

OF THE HEART

THE CARESS AND THE HURT

For Kenneth Andrews Keeney
May 20, 1909 – June 6, 1984

When I gave you my first poems long ago,
You wrote these words: "I love your poetry.
It strikes some deep-hidden bit of my heart with a touch
That is half a caress, half a hurt. There are few things
That strike that deep . . . but when I read the one —
The one you gave me first down on the bridge —
I felt for a moment as though I must choke. I had
To fight down a lump in my throat that would not go.
Perhaps you can understand . . . can you?"

Of course
I could understand. This was high praise. Your words —
Ingenuous, uncritical, but dear —
Have kept me searching all my life for words
To capture the caress, the hurt life brings . . .

And so — since I can give you little else —
Once more here at the last I give you words.

THE LILY DISHES

Today Mother gave me the lily dishes — handed them to me one by one from the square-fronted oak china closet that has always stood in her dining room. One by one I wrapped them in newspapers, packed them in sturdy boxes, brought them home. The lily dishes — made in England before the first World War, each thin white piece encircled with pale green lily pads, each circle interspersed with delicate pink-and-white blossoms. It didn't seem right to take them. The china closet looked bare without them. They had been there fifty-seven years.

"Millie gave them to me, dear, the week before you were born. My Christmas present. We'd had a lot of snow that year. I remember I worried the doctor wouldn't be able to get through when I needed him for you. Millie hauled the wooden box home on a sled from the Center Street carline — a good mile. The carline stopped at Garland Street then . . ."

"Did you unwrap them that night?"

"No, Millie hid them in the barn. I didn't even know about them. You know we always had our presents Christmas morning. I was big as a barrel, of course, couldn't lean over to unpack them. His mother came in and helped me . . ."

My mother's voice trailed away. She is eighty-four now, white-haired, frail, but her eyes are the same intense blue as the eyes of the young girl-mother in the painting that hangs on my wall. I could see her that Christmas morning — thin-faced, vibrant, hard-working, already the mother of two boys — Merle, four, and Lloyd, who had been born on Christmas Day two years before. She would undoubtedly have been up early that morning, baked Lloyd a birthday cake . . .

"Your grandmother was so excited," she went on. "Pulled the straw off each piece and held it up to the light. 'Oh, Clara,' she'd say, 'aren't they beautiful! Two platters, and a gravy boat! What a lovely big pitcher, and see here — the cups are two sizes!' The big ones must be for coffee, I told her, and the small ones for tea. She washed two small ones right then and there, put the kettle on, and we had our first cup of tea!"

"Did you have a piece of Lloydie's birthday cake along with it?"

"Don't remember that, dear, but I remember I was wild to use the whole set — 100 pieces! Couldn't, of course. You were due any day. I used them first on your father's birthday, the last day of March. Invited the American Express boys and had a sledding party. Your father had that big bob sled with the bell on the front — it held twenty-six people . . .'"

And mother's voice trailed off again. Millie Coffin was to have only fifteen more birthdays, Grandmother Eva Pomroy Coffin only three, but Clara could not see into the future that long-ago morning. Rich in happiness, she was looking forward to the child. Perhaps, after two boys, it would be a girl. Millie would like that. He had no sister — no girls on the Coffin side. If it was a girl, Millie would probably spoil her.

I was born six days after Christmas, December 3l, 1910. I was a girl. I was most certainly spoiled.

The lily dishes were a happy part of all my growing-up years. On every Thanksgiving, Christmas, Easter, Fourth of July, on every family birthday, whenever 'company' came, the fragile cups, saucers, plates would be taken carefully from the oak china closet, used to set the long oak table in the dining room. Until I was six, I could look and admire but not touch the pink-and-white lilies. Then, at the Annual Sunday School picnic that year, I picked my first real pond lilies, and the next morning I was allowed to arrange them in the beautiful lily dish nappy . . . .

We were lucky to have a picnic that year. It was almost called off — because of a hymn! We were not really a church, or even a Sunday School. We were just the dozen or so families living along Outer Broadway — Methodists, Baptists, Episcopalians, one or two Roman Catholics, and a few non-believers who came for the sociability. We met every Sunday afternoon in the one-room Hillside School to read a chapter from the Bible, say the Lord's Prayer, and sing hymns. There was always much more singing than reading and praying. My father, the 'superintendent,' would stand behind the teacher's desk on the raised platform and invite us to call out the numbers. The singing was loud, toes tapped, feet swung, and everyone had a good time.

We all knew each other's favorites. Papa usually called on George Noddin first, because George always wanted *"Revive Us Again by the Power of the Blood,"* and that is a good lively one to start with. John Boober, sure he was going to die soon, always called for *"When the Roll Is Called Up Yonder, I'll Be There!"* He did die soon, and we all went to his funeral. I can still see his open casket, kitty-cornered across his front parlor and filling half the room. Mr. Boober, white and still, looked strange against white satin, and I wondered if the roll had been called up yonder yet. His was the first funeral I ever went to on Outer Broadway, but not the last.

Mamie Hillman always called for *"In the Garden."* She liked to sing: *'And he walks with me, and he talks with me, and he tells me I am his own . . .'* Bill Greene would tease her. "That's the old maid's hymn, Mamie! Don't forget you've got five kids!" When my father was happy, he'd call for *"There is Power, Power, Everlasting Power in the Precious Blood of the Lamb."* I knew Papa wanted power to give up smoking and be a Methodist like Mama. Methodists weren't allowed to smoke. Papa tried to stop, but he never could, so most often he'd call for *"Almost Persuaded,"* or *"Just as I Am."* In the first one he was telling Mama not to give up on him, maybe he could still be persuaded, but in the second he was saying, "I can't change, Lord. If you want me, you can have me, but you'll have to take me just as I am."

The reason we almost didn't have the Sunday School Picnic that year was on account of Mrs. Foster and the war and the hymn Rose Davenport called for. Everyone knew Mrs. Foster's son, Alton, had enlisted and gone overseas with General Pershing. He'd been 'Missing in Action' since Easter, but in spite of that Mrs. Davenport called for *"Where Is My Wandering Boy Tonight,"* and we all started singing it at the top of our voices. Mrs. Foster squeezed out from behind her school desk and hurried out, daubing her eyes. Papa signaled the pianist right away to change to *"Does Jesus Care?"* but Mrs. Foster kept on going.

"Louder," Papa urged. "Louder on the chorus!" We sang with all our might — *"Oh, yes, he cares! I know he cares! His heart is touched with my grief!"* but Mrs. Foster kept teetering on up the hill toward her big house at the top.

Mama was angry. "That was Rose Davenport, did that," she told Papa as we walked home. "I sat right beside her and heard her. She never did like Alton —"

"Oh, she didn't mean any harm, dear. Just thoughtless —"

"Thoughtless my foot! Maybe we shouldn't even have the picnic this year. Mrs. Foster feels so bad —"

"Thirty kids would feel bad if we didn't have the picnic, Clara! You just have the chicken sandwiches and lemonade ready Saturday morn —"

"Lemonade!" Mama sputtered. "Do you remember what happened to the lemonade last year? It was a long way from lemonade before the day was over — and it was Rose Davenport did that, too!"

Papa took a cigar out of his Sunday suit pocket, lit it. Mama moved a foot or two away from him. "Rose isn't a Methodist, Clara, like you. She's young, lively, and Irish." Papa blew a perfect smoke ring into the Sunday air. "A few drops of Irish whiskey may be a sin to you, dear, but it isn't to Rose. She's a good Roman Catholic." Mama sniffed and had the last word.

"It was more than a few drops last year, and Irish or not, whiskey doesn't belong at a Sunday School picnic. You just keep Rose Davenport away from my jugs!"

So Papa promised to keep an eye on the lemonade, and on Friday Lloyd and I chased the chickens round and round the yard till Merle caught two and chopped off their heads with his hatchet. Only then would Mama come out, carrying two pails of hot water from the tank at the back of the Clarion stove, plunge the still-wiggling birds into the steaming bath and strip their feathers — every feather to be saved for a mattress or a pillow. The chickens were gutted and hung up to cool. Hours later, Mama mixed bread, onion, sage, and melted butter for her famous stuffing, filled the birds to a plumpness never known in life, sewed the openings with strong white thread, and lifted the roasting pan into the oven.

"Fill the woodbox," she ordered Lloyd and Merle, "and keep the fire up. I have to lie down awhile." Tears would be streaming down Mama's cheeks as she went upstairs. Always when she fixed chickens, Mama would cry. For years I thought it was because she felt bad about the chickens. After all, she had carried the eggs up the ladder to the hayloft, put the setting hen on them, watched the baby chicks peck their way out of the shell and grow from pale yellow to dark Rhode Island Red, fed and watered them morning and night for months, and then — the hatchet and the oven. Only

when we were grown did we learn about allergies and discover that feathers, not feelings, caused mother's headaches.

Saturday came at last. The roasted chickens had been cooled, carved, and put between thick slices of homemade bread, the lemonade jugs stowed carefully on the newmown hay in the long wagons. We climbed aboard, ten to fifteen to a wagon depending on our size, and paraded out Broadway — past the Greenes, the Hillmans, the Noddins, the Ranletts, past Mrs. Foster's house on the hill, every shade drawn, past my Aunt Fanny Barker's.

Aunt Fanny, short, squat, Indian-featured, was hoeing her corn. "Have a good time at Pushaw!" she called, and I remembered that her mother had been Priscilla Pushaw before she married my great-great-grandfather, Cap'n Gulliver. This was the family pond we were going to. No wonder Millie Coffin didn't want to cancel the picnic. No wonder he knew just how to build a roaring fire once we got there — how to toss in potatoes and unhusked corn, pull them out roasted just right. My father was one-eighth Indian, and I was one-sixteenth.

Best of all, Papa loved to be on the water. Hour after hour he loaded children who had seldom been in a boat into the largest one there, rowed them patiently out, around, back to the rickety, unpainted dock, but I did not go. Papa had promised me something special. My ride was to be in a canoe, not a boat.

"See there? Way off in that cove? That's where the water lilies are, Clarine — like the ones on Mama's best dishes. We'll go over there after I give the other children their rides. You and I'll go in the canoe."

So I waited. All around me grew the common wild flowers of Maine — Queen Anne's lace, black-eyed Susans, Indian paintbrush — but I did not pick any. I was going to pick lilies!

"Millie, you're not taking that child in that leaky old canoe!"

"Have to go by canoe, dear. Too shallow for a boat. Sit on the bottom, Clarine. Hold onto the sides."

"She can't even swim —"

"I can, dear. Don't worry!"

My father sat in the stern. I twisted my head to see him. The paddle flashed in and out, silent except for the quiet drip of a few drops now and then. I felt the canoe surge forward under me and turned my head again.

"Sit still, honey. See the lily pads? We're getting close."

And we were. A wonderful fragrance filled the air. On all sides floated huge round, green pads and in among them, lifting pure white faces to the sun, the water lilies.

"We're just in time," Papa said. "They're beginning to close. They're a morning flower — but we'll pick the buds, too. They'll all open out in the morning." He reached out time and again, pulling up long stems from the muddy bottom and tossing lily after lily into the canoe.

"You pick some, too. See that big one? I'll paddle close and you stretch — don't fall in! Mama'd never forgive me —"

We came close, but I was not quick enough. The canoe passed over the lily.

"Try again . . . I'll lift it up on the paddle. Grab quick!" I got on my knees in the wet bottom and stretched both hands far over the edge. My father manoevered the canoe, the paddle. Suddenly I could grasp the flower. I tugged hard. The white head came off in my hands. No stem.

"Good for you! You've picked your first pond lily. Smell it, honey!" I lifted the pure white petals to my nose, breathed deep.

"It smells beautiful."

"Wrong word," my father laughed. "You're supposed to say 'heavenly' — that's what Mama always says — 'heavenly.'"

"Is that because we have lilies on Easter, when Jesus went to heaven?"

"Don't know about that, honey, but you hold a lily under your Mama's nose when we get back, and you'll see —"

I held the stemless lily under Mama's nose. She breathed deep, smiled at me and then across at Papa.

"Heavenly," she said and breathed deep again. I knew Papa had given Mama her lily dishes just before I was born. When I smelled the lilies that day, I knew why she liked her dishes so much. "Roll up the stems and put them in the empty lemonade jug. Lloyd, fill the jug with lake water and set it in our wagon."

The day went fast. Mama began to talk about going home. Tired of horse shoes and baseball, the men sat around the long picnic tables, talking and laughing. Someone was playing a harmonica, and Rose Davenport climbed up on a table and began to dance an Irish jig. The men clapped and laughed louder than ever. I wondered if Rose had done it again to the lemonade.

Red lanterns on either side of the hay wagons had to be lit before we got back to Hillside School. The horses were tired. Men and big boys jumped down from the wagons and walked alongside as we climbed the steep hill above Bean's Store. I could hear my Papa singing *"There is Power, Power,"* so I knew he was happy. The stars came out.

Papa dropped back when it was quite dark and put his hand on the side of the wagon where I sat clutching my gallon jug of lilies.

"Had a good time?" He whispered because the babies were asleep all around me.

"Heavenly," I whispered back.

"See the Big Dipper, honey — right over there? And there's Orion . . . Can you find the Little Dipper, too?" I looked hard, but I could not find another dipper.

"Tip your head way back on the hay — see? Right there!"

I found it at last and smiled at him. "Heavenly," I whispered again. Papa patted my shoulder and walked on.

I tried to keep my eyes on the Little Dipper, but they would not stay open. Tomorrow, I was sure, Mama would let me touch the lily dishes. She'd open the glass doors in the oak china closet, take out the round nappy with its wreath of green pads and pink-and-white blossoms, give it to me for my lilies. *I'll put my green pads around the edge,* I thought, *white flowers in the middle. Papa said they'd all open out in the morning.*

Today mother gave me the lily dishes — handed them to me one by one from the square-fronted oak china closet . . . one by one I wrapped them, brought them home . . . and here, hundreds of miles away in my own home as I unwrap them, one by one the memories come flooding back — memories of another place, another time . . . of a father, a mother who loved each other, loved and cared for their children . . . of a religion for all ages, all faiths in a one-room schoolhouse on Sunday afternoons . . . of new-mown hay in slow-moving wagons . . . of pond lilies in my hands as I searched for stars . . . and of a voice I knew — strong, sure, happy — singing up to those stars: *"There is Power, Power, Everlasting Power . . . ."*

Thank you, Mama . . . for giving me the lily dishes.

FAMILY FUN

Mother saved all year
to take six children to the Bangor Fair
where we each paid a dime to lean over a pit
        *watch the **Wild Man of Borneo***
        with black, matted hair
        wearing only a leopard-skin loin cloth
struggle and strain to break thick chains
bound round his hands, his arms, his legs
        giving all the while
        great agonizing growls, blood-curdling screams
that we heard over and over again in nightmares
        way up till Christmas . . . .

*Father said, **"Tide's out! Let's go clamming!"***
took us to the ocean to squish hot feet
        in cool mud flats
fish up fat clams with bare black hands
squeeze them hard to make them squirt
souse the slatted basket up and down in white surf
        steam them under seaweed
        over driftwood fires
brought us home at dusk with black fingernails
        pockets full of clam shells
        bellies full of clams . . . .

Mother dressed us in starched white linen
rode us fifteen miles from Bangor to Oldtown
on 'the oldest railroad in the USA'
to stay overnight with our rich Aunt Lillie
        who had no children
        gave us one cookie each for our dessert
and when she showed us her big front parlor
        where the conch shells were
        and the dried cocoanuts, and the ivory fans
and all the other things brought from China long ago
kept saying over and over again:
        "Don't touch! Don't touch! Don't touch!"

*Father said, **"Blackberries are ripe! Fetch lard pails!"***

16

walked us across warm meadows
>*yellow with goldenrod, orange with Susans*
>*blue with asters, red with paintbrush*
showed us how to whistle on a blade of grass
suck a piece of timothy when we were thirsty
carried the youngest home on his back
gave us all big dishes of his berries for our supper
>*to eat with yellow cream*
>*purple tongues, purple teeth*
because ours had all disappeared on the way . . . .

Mother wound our hair in white cotton rags
brushed corkscrew curls around her finger
fastened white ribbon hairbows on each head
buttoned shoes too small on feet too big
>*walked us long miles*
>*all the way downtown to Perry's Studio*
>*where a man put a beautiful toy in our hands*
>*a white-painted horse*
with red-painted wheels and a horsehair tail
>*for just one minute*
while he went under a big black cloth, yelled
>**"Smile! Look happy!"**
and sent us limping home in our too-small shoes . . . .

And yellowing away in a drawer somewhere
I have the picture of that solemn child
>*with the stiff, tight curls*
>*and the high-buttoned shoes*
>*clutching the toy that wasn't hers*
And when I come across it, I think of the mother
>*who worked so hard, so very hard*
>*to give six children all the things*
>*they didn't need and didn't want . . . .*

But the picture of the child
with purple tongue, muddy hands
wild curls tangled with breezes from the sea
tossed high in the air by a laughing Dad
caught, held safe in strong, sure arms
>*that picture I look at often and smile because*
>*it is in my heart, shiny and bright forever . . . .*

WHEN WORK WAS PLAY

Sometimes, looking back, I think we six Coffin kids growing up on Outer Broadway a half-century ago must have been stupid. Really stupid. We didn't know the difference between work and play. Grown-ups worked us like little demons to get what they wanted done, and all the time we thought we were having fun.

Take, for example, my great-great Aunt Fanny's pumpkin pies. I thought of her today as I watched a mother with a little girl pick a pumpkin pie out of the frozen food bin at the supermarket. Plop the pie in the oven, turn the dial to BAKE, and an hour later cut and serve. Not so my Aunt Fanny. She may have been in her 90's, but she still grew her own. We worked six months for a piece of her pumpkin pie and didn't even know it.

Work started in late April, the day we heard the ice was going out at Pushaw Pond. That was the day the winter-starved fish would bite like fury. We'd all — Merle, Lloyd, Jill, Millard, Bart, and I — been digging worms for days from the still half-frozen dirt. We were ready.

We hitched Old Maude to the rickety wagon, and she reluctantly hauled the six of us up Foster's Hill, past Sanfords and Emerys, then down the other side to the Burleigh Road, over to Essex, and left to Gould's Landing. Six long miles against a strong east wind. There we watched the little channel on the far side of the lake widen. Big cracks in the frozen pond split into smaller and smaller ones, closer and closer together, until huge chunks of ice slipped silently beneath the inky water.

"Why," asked Bart, "do you say the ice goes out? It doesn't go out. It goes down."

"Get in the boat," Merle ordered, "and start bailing. She's leaking like a sieve."

Hard work to bail the icy water, to hold the boat against the wind, to untangle the snarled lines, to thread the slimy earthworms on the hooks. Hard work, but nobody told us. All for Aunt Fanny's Thanksgiving pies in the far distant future.

Because my Aunt Fanny was half-Indian. Her father may have been Captain Benjamin Gulliver who sailed his small ship from Scotland up the Penobscot to Bangor, largest lumber port in the world, and built the first small house on Outer Broadway, but her mother was Priscilla Pushaw, full-blooded Penobscot Indian, for whose family this very pond was named.

And so Aunt Fanny must have a bass or a pickerel or a couple of yellow perch at the bottom of every hill of corn, around which, of course, she grew pumpkins for her pies. So we fished till dark. We caught Aunt Fanny's organic fertilizer and, singing and hollering, with raw red hands and runny noses, carried dozens of fish home to her in triumph — and didn't even know we'd been working.

We even thought it was fun to plant the garden. Merle hoed deep holes in the stubborn soil. Lloyd tossed in the fish. I picked kernels of corn from last year's ears. Jill counted them out. Millard dropped them in the holes, and Bart generously circled each hill with pumpkin seeds. Then, whooping and hollering as Aunt Fanny instructed us, 1/16th Indian that we were, we jumped up and down on the hills to tamp in the soil until the garden was smooth as glass. We expended untold energy, and all the while we thought we were playing.

So Aunt Fanny got her garden planted, and during hot July and hotter August she got it watered the same happy way.

"Why don't you children have a water fight — it's so hot! Here, haul up the bucket and chase each other through the corn." The old rope squeaked and groaned as we nearly emptied the well, drenching each other and the parched corn as we raced up and down the rows. Such stupid kids, to think such tedious toil was fun.

Come October, Aunt Fanny let us have all the corn stalks in her garden for our school Hallowe'en Party. We sawed away at every stalk and carted the heavy load down the road to Hillside School. We left her garden clean as a whistle, for she let us have the pumpkins, too, overnight, for Jack o' Lanterns.

Our arms ached, scooping out pulp and seeds from dozens of Aunt Fanny's great pumpkins. We had three or four grinning faces on every windowsill in the school and carried the heaviest one we could lift for our very own. The day after Hallowe'en we brought them all back to Aunt Fanny, cleaned and ready to can. She also told us to bring her any extra ones we found along the way. She was, after all, half Scotch. Soon dozens of yellow jars lined her windowsills.

Wednesday before Thanksgiving, Hillside School let out at noon. We six Coffin kids raced up Broadway, dropped our books at 782, and on up the hill to the little white house, nestled now in the shadow of WLBZ's antenna. Today Aunt Fanny baked her Thanksgiving pies, and we could have some. No waiting till tomorrow. The filling would be ready — oh, cinnamon! oh, clove and ginger! oh, sweet, thick blackstrap! — the filling would be ready, and we could taste it raw!

Of course, there'd still be a few small tasks.

"Run over to Hillman's, Merle. Bring back this pail of cream. Clarine and Lillian, carry these jars down cellar and put them on the shelves — careful! Millie and Bart, help Lloyd fill the woodbox. Takes lots of wood to bake pies!"

So we laughed and ran and sweated and worked, the smell of bubbling spices urging us on each time we passed the oven door, right up to the very moment when at last, at last, April to November, we sat down, the six of us, around Aunt Fanny's black walnut table and watched her cut for each of us a huge, generous, warm, fragrant, golden wedge of pumpkin pie. It was Thanksgiving, and we were truly thankful.

Wily, wily old Scots-Indian aunt, to work us so hard, when we thought we were playing! Stupid, stupid Coffin kids, not to know the difference!

Or were we all really very, very smart?

*Reprinted from the **Bangor Daily News***

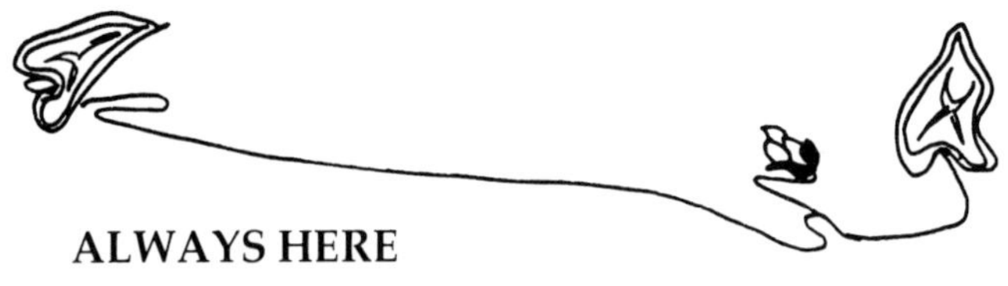

ALWAYS HERE

Always here — the lake, the hills, the sky . . .
Sweet smell of pine cones, roasting in the sun . . .
Always here — the lone loon's aching cry . . .
Twin stars, above, below, when day is done . . .

Always here — the peepers' symphony,
The circling gulls, the eagles' swooping flight . . .
Always here — the lilies' mystery,
Up from black mud come blooms of purest white . . .

When far away in cities built by man,
Man's suffering, sin, and sorrow ever near,
I shall be glad, remembering again,
The lake, the hills, the sky are always here.

Plantation 33
Long Pond, Maine, 1937

SOMEONE

For William Heagan Goodell, Jr.

Someone remembers you when you were young —
Closes her eyes and sees you hurrying
Along a college walk to take her hand
And run through scurrying leaves for fun.

Someone
Hears laughter echoing across the years
As, lifting her high to keep pink slippers dry,
You stride through drifts of swirling snow.

Someone
Walks time and again with you across the bridge,
Twisting a bit of lilac picked in rain,
Time and again in popcorn-scented dark
Sits marveling at films that talk.

Someone
In sporty little cars with rumble seats
Still rides on summer nights inside your arm
Or waltzes there to medleys long unplayed,
Still dips and sways, still feels on cheek and hair
The brush of lips, whispering you care.

Someone —
Oh, know, my very dear, though time must pass,
The seasons come and go, steps slow, eyes dim—
Someone still sees you in the same old way.
Someone remembers you and loves you still.
Someone remembers you and will until
The fading music dies, the song is sung.
Someone remembers you — gallant, and young!

Reprinted from the **Maine Alumnus**

COINCIDENTAL DAY

April 3, 1931

It was, of course, by chance we met that day.
By happenstance — an unexpected cut,
Some stationery needed, bookstore near,
And there you were, standing with book in hand,
A tall, slim boy I'd known through college years
Only by name, quite casually. You turned,
Put book back on the shelf, said "Hi," and smiled.
"Oh, hi — what are you reading?"
*   "Anything —*
Except religion. I've no use for that."
"An atheist, then?"
*   "Almost —" And so we talked*
Awhile of God, condescendingly, until
The clerk put stationery in my hand.
"Must go — write a letter for the mail."

*   All chance,*
Of course. All happenstance. And did He smile ,
The Omniscient One, that coincidental day,
As we dismissed him in our cavalier way —
And is He smiling still? — hearing you say
Offhandedly, "I'll walk along with you
A little way, if I may . . . a little way . . . ."

April 3, 1981

I NEVER KNEW

I never knew of love
Until
That night in May beneath the stars
When misty moonlight drifted through
The needles of the pines
And older needles, brown and scented, made for us
A warm and fragrant bed . . .

I never knew of love
Until
Upon my full warm breast you laid
The fullness of your lips and swore that you were mine
While high and sweet the peepers played
Our wedding march
For I married you then
Your soul and mine in holy radiance and bliss
Became as one . . .

It matters not
What other man may place
A golden circlet on my hand . . .
I have been bride
To you and you alone
Are my true mate . . .
Through all the years close-pressed
Adored
I love you

SONG OF THE VIKING'S DAUGHTER

And will I marry you, my love,
And will I e'er be true?
I cannot tell, my love, until
I see the sea with you . . .

Until I stand beside your side
To hear great breakers roar
In endless foaming impotence
Against the endless shore . . .

Until I lie beside your side
To watch the white gulls write
Their lovely curving messages
Across the sky in white . . .

Until I know that your heart swells
As mine with almost pain
To feel the wind fill out a sail
And give it life again . . .

For Viking blood is in my veins,
In my heart wanderlust!
Since I shall love the sea alway,
The man I marry must!

And will I marry you, my love,
And will I e'er be true?
I cannot tell, my love, until
I see the sea with you.

Reprinted from **Renaissance**

THE LIGHTS OF LOVE

I met you in the sunlight, love,
One April day, all green, all blue.
The sunbeams seemed to dance with you,
Entranced with you, as I was, too,
When first we met, my love!

We laughed beneath the starlight, love,
Flinging our gladness to the sky,
Knowing our love could never die.
We heard the stars on high reply
When first we laughed, my love!

By moonlight we first kissed, my love,
A kiss so soft upon my hair
The west wind might have left it there.
A token from the fairest fair
In all the world, my love!

In candlelight we married, love.
I see again the tall flames shine.
I hear again the vow divine
That made thee mine, and me all thine
For all the years, my love!

By firelight we'll grow old, my love,
Your hand in mine for aye and aye
Until all earth lights fade away
In dawning ray of endless day
When we are old, my love!

Reprinted from the **Bangor Daily News**

ON MONUMENTS

We lay on the riverbank that final day,
Remembering the springtime hours we'd shared,
Counting them one by one, and reaching out
Pried pebbles from wet sand, one for each hour . . .
Like playful children then laid stone on stone
Until we'd built a kind of pyramid —
Uneven, frail, a fragile monument
To youth and joy and love, to hopes and dreams
Far off, more fragile still — then clasping hands,
Kissed lightly one last time and walked away.

The world has countless monuments — Stonehenge,
Sphinx, Eiffel Tower, the marble David white
In the bright Italian square, the supine slave
That altered Schweitzer's life, the Taj Mahal . . .

Why, then, when I think of monuments, do I
See only a little heap of tide-washed stones,
Wavery, unsure, a wobbly pyramid
Built long ago by an artless boy and girl
Who count shared hours, then kiss, and hand in hand,
Their faces toward each other, walk away . . . .

LIGHTED HOURS

We shared together only simple joys —
The moonlit sea, red sunset through the trees,
A certain star — for always strangely sweet
And natural seemed our two souls' company.
Our love was not for words. Only to know
The aching grip of strong, lean hands sufficed,
Or meet your eyes across the candlelight
And feel myself like flame-touched wax dissolve.

It may be we shall never meet again,
But I'll remember you. Though many days
And scenes both near and far shall come between,
I'll not forget. Life brings its lighted hours
Whose loveliness and warmth into the gloom
Of soon-forgotten things fade not away.

So on all mountain tops and by all seas
And when all ships creep silent past the moon,
I'll think of you and love you tenderly.

ONCE

We had it once
The joy, the walk-on-air
The oh-what-a-wonderful-world, the ecstasy
All ours
A few brief halcyon days
And if
We lost it there
Somewhere
Along the way
No matter, dear
Be glad
We had it once.

JAPE

Gods on your mountains, were you bored with all
Life's other merry jests that you should please —
When I was peaceful, when I was content —
To lift me for one windswept day into
Your radiant company, show me all light,
All laughter, and all love only to tire
Of my too naive joy and fling me back
Into the commonplace?

And was it as a kind of souvenir
Or payment for your quite amusing jape
That you should leave upreaching empty arms
And eyes from viewing light too bright struck blind?

O gods, I do not beg. Too well I know
That life on mountain heights is yours, not mine.
This only tell: why was I shown the light?
And how, knowing what life could be, am I
To live it as it all too surely is?

28

ASTRONOMY I — THE LONG, LONG COURSE

The first time ever we walked beneath the stars —
A million stars, a million years ago —
You stretched your arm straight up and gave me one:
"That's our star! Two points off the bow of Delta Tau!"
Then swung my arm round till I found it, too.
"By the triangle?"
                        "No, sweet! Not a triangle!
Just two big stars and a little one — ha, ha!"

So we argued names, discarded Latin, Greek,
Chose a simple honest name and nickname, too,
*And you said, **"Now hang on, sweet! Hold tight! Tonight***
We'll fly right up and say 'Hello' to Osc!"

So you kissed me then, and up, up, up we flew
Past a million other stars to claim our own —
'For better or for worse, for rich or poor,
***In sickness, health'** — till we kissed our last goodbye.*
"Don't say 'Goodbye' — say 'See you later, dear!'
When you look at Oscar, I'll be looking, too!"

So I looked . . . and looked . . . through a million lonely nights,
*Humming Hoagy's song: **'Sometimes I wonder why —'***
Looked 'two points off the bow' when Delta Tau
Was a million, million lonely miles away . . .

And so, my sweet, were you, and I never did
***'See you later, dear,'** and, no, there never was*
***'A little one — ha, ha!'** Still, I had a star.*
I had a star. I always had a star.
Good times or bad, glad times or sad, always
I had a star. I had a special star —
A special, distant, cold, uncaring star
That a faithless sweetheart picked from a million stars
And gave with a faithless kiss on an April night
A million, million, million years ago . . . .

NEVER A JUNE

Never a June but I remember, dear,
When pine trees lift white candles to the sky
And leaves unfurl, all new, all tender green,
Never a June when lilac blooms but I
Remember — once I called you, and you came.

I called you once in need, in blinding hurt
None but the very young can ever know —
Never a June but I remember, dear —
I called you once in turmoil, and you came . . .
Came instantly, asking no questions, made
A world within the circle of your arms,
A world all safe, wherein I was enclosed.

Never a June when leaves hang tremblingly
And lilac bloom perfumes the warm, sweet air,
But I remember, dear, you held me close
Until my heart was stilled against your own,
And smoothed my hair, and kissed my tears away
On such a day, on such a bright June day . . .

Never a June when tapers on the pines,
All slim, all slender white, light up the sky,
But I remember, dear, though other Junes
Have come and gone and I have solace found
In other arms than yours . . .

                    Never a June
Till no leaf stir for me, nor lilac bloom,
And candles can no longer light my dark,
Never a June but I'll remember, dear —
I called you once in anguish and in pain.
I called you — and you came, you came, you came.

BELIEVERS

*When Lorni was five, I took her to see **Peter Pan,***
And as, leaning forward, perched on the edge of her seat,
She clapped wildly, wildly, that Tinker Bell live, not die,
Suddenly, in that very moment, dear,
After years of forgetting, I remembered you —
The only man I ever knew who believed
In fairies, too —
          Queen Mab, Titania, all
Puck's mischievous madcap crew were real to you,
Wee folk we only feel, not see, in mist,
Moonbeam, rainbow, and tree —

                    ***"Clap!"** Peter begged,*
A sob in his husky voice as the tiny light
Grew fainter, flickered, died . . .
                    "Clap! If you
***Believe!"** And I felt my daughter tug my sleeve —*
***"Clap harder, Mommy! Harder, please!"** Blue eyes*
Ablaze with fear and tears, she beat small hands
Together frantically . . .

               ***She believes,** I thought,*
***She could be his child, his spirit child . . .** and felt*
My own tears, burning hot, and then I, too,
Leaned forward, clapping wildly, wildly, not —
For fairies, but for days we knew when life
Was young, and love was true, and I believed
With all my heart — yes, I believed in you.

LETTER

> *Isn't it strange —*
How your remembered script, so long unseen,
Can startle, make the heart beat faster, take
Me decades back in one quick glance to young —
Not mother, wife, grandmother, only young . . .
Untouched, your hands still shyly tentative . . .
Lips innocent, unkissed . . . all unexplored,
Unlived, the pulse to come . . .

> *Isn't it strange —*
How such a common thing, plain white, addressed
In ordinary blue, postmarked in black,
Can change slow steps that cautious creep about
To flying feet of schoolgirl, racing home
To find this in the post . . .

> *Isn't it strange —*
The way you write my name can move me still,
Each upward stroke, each curve call back the hands
That stroked each curve . . .

> *Now break the seal. Take out*
The pages that suffice to tell a life —
Advanced degree, long marriage, work, the war,
Vacations, travel, health — recounted here
With courteous restraint, as to someone
Remote . . . almost unknown . . . a stranger, yes —
We've lived our lives apart. I watch the sun
Rise each day from one sea. You watch it sink
Into another. Still — is it not strange
That for a little space of glad surprise
Your old familiar writing could blot out
The miles, the years, efface dull age, erase
Both time and space?

> *Dear long-ago first love,*
Is it not strange — and strangely wonderful —
That flesh does not forget, remembers yet?
That love, once freely given, does not die?
Lives on unfed . . . unnourished still endures?

TOUCH

You have not touched my hand in many years
Nor smoothed my hair nor brushed away my tears,
But, when the letters come, I lay my face
On letters your familiar hand has traced
And almost feel across long years, far lands
The still-remembered touch, the gentle hands.

KEY

"Keep this until I come again," *you said*
And pressed into my hand a small gold key,
Emblazoned with a tree, and went away
And did not come again.

Long years it lay
Against the velvet of my jewel box —
Unclaimed, unworn, unused.

Who would have thought
This small gold key had power to unlock
A friendship frozen in oblivion,
Leap decades of divergence, reconcile
Two hearts — grown older, wiser — each to each?

"DON'T CRY!"

He cried easily those last few years — the sound
Of the children's voices on the telephone,
A hymn his mother sang, an old snapshot,
My hand on his in a crowded restaurant —
"Don't cry!" *I'd say impatiently.* **"Oh, please —**
Don't cry!"
                Retired — pride, vigor, usefulness
All gone — he laid the masks aside and cried.

'Second childhood,' some would say, and in a way
He was a child, more sensitive, his 'heart
Upon his sleeve,' more easily hurt or pleased . . .

Like a child he'd bring the first half-open bloom
From the lilac hedge, hold it delightedly
Under my nose, say **"Smell!"** *Or shuffle out*
Day after day in June until he'd found
On unpruned bushes planted long ago,
A stunted rose . . . **"Don't cry! Oh, please — don't cry!"**

Don't cry . . . I tell myself, longing to see
Those childlike tears . . . have rosebuds brought to me . . .

PEREGRINE WIDOW

"Where is your home?" *they ask — strangers, polite,*
Well-meaning, wanting to be kind. *"Where do*
You live?" *"Where are you from?"*
                                    I do not know.
I am from a husband's heart that held me close
Long years and holds me now no more. I am from
The life, the love we shared, the homes, the rooms
Where laughter ranᵍ and tears were kissed away,
From rocking chairs where lullabies were sung
And small ones comforted, from fires that burn,
From flowers that bloom no longer, candlelight
On tables set with silver, altar rails
Where hands I knew broke the forgiving bread —
I am from all these, for they are gone away,
Receded quite, all passed . . . and I am from . . .

"Where are you from?" *they ask.* *"Where do you live?"*
They ask and ask again, *"Where is your home?"*
There is no home — an address, yes, a house,
Table and chair and bed and board, but when
The heart is homeless, then there is no home,
And I am from . . .

                    "Where are you from? Where is
Your home? Where do you live?"
                                    I do not live,
But go through motions only day by day —
Rise up, lie down, walk, talk, say 'yea' and 'nay' —
Living is something I did yesterday.
I am from . . . I am from . . . I am from . . . I am away.

Kansas City
Christmas, 1981

CLAH-RA-INE

Playful, you change my name to Navajo.
Will you then be my shaman? Paint for me
Bright images in sands of memory?
Pound into powdered rock our yesterdays?
Call down old gods? Depict the great events —
Your word, your touch, the laughter in your eyes —
That changed a life? Work holy charms that cure?

I am in need of healing. Bending low,
Here at the circle's edge I bow me down,
Wounded in spirit, broken . . . make me whole!
Grant me the central place, the heart's deep core . . .
Enfold me, hold me there a little time
And make for me the magic mandala . . . .

Let twirling fingers swirl the colored sands —
Draw darkness, light . . . red sunset, dawn . . . white mist
In deepest canyon, high on mountain peak,
Above still pool, on crashing waterfall . . .
Oh, reconcile the harsh polarities!
Draw ice! Draw fire! Rejection and desire!
Show thunder in the snow, warm springtime rain . . .
Show blossoming tree and windblown, dying leaf . . .
Meeting and parting . . . pain and ecstasy . . .
Great eagle, soaring, small bird near at hand . . .
Firefly ephemeral, far steadfast star . . .
And sing with star, bird, tree the age-old chant —
The song of joy the morning stars began!
The song of love that made the universe!

Thus seeing, hearing, I may yet be well,
May rise from death to life healed by the touch
Of old shared memory, may walk again
The shimmering rainbow trail . . .
                                    I ask because
You change my name and call me Navajo —
And walked the trail with me once long ago.

NOT TRUE

You say you can't remember, dear, that I
*Must have forgotten, too, the **where,** the **why,***
*The **when** of how we fell in love, we two —*
          Not true, not true.

Here in old age, you say, I can't recall
A certain bridge, a certain waterfall,
A night beside the sea when our love grew —
          Not true, not true.

I must, you say, have written it somewhere,
The feeling of your lips upon my hair,
The tender touch of hands that I once knew —
          Not true, not true.

I must have quite forgotten, too, you say,
The way your laughter rang, the endearing way
Your voice broke when you first said, "I love you —"
          Not true, not true.

But — will I remember till the day I die
Our sweet, young love, and do I wish that I
Could sometimes share that memory with you?
          Now that, my love, is true. All true.

LET ME WALK WITH YOU

*Let me walk with you sometimes when you walk alone
On summer days, my hand inside your arm . . .
Imagine me there, my step matching your own,
The sun on our faces, radiant and warm.*

*Only one plume of breath will rise in the frosty night
If I come with you when the harvest moon hangs low;
Only one set of footprints show in the pristine white
If together we go through softly falling snow.*

*Do not pause alone by the darkening wood to hear
In the springtime dusk the hidden whippoorwill.
Do not wait alone for the first pale star to appear
As the last red glow fades slowly from the hill.*

*Let me walk with you. None but you will know I am there —
Only turn when you hear your name and touch my hair.*

WISH

I wish someone would come along and fling
An arm around my shoulders, leave it there
Awhile, unthinkingly, till I reach up
And press a hand, a hand that presses back . . .

Nothing I touch responds — not wooden arms
On rocking chair . . . not stiff, unbending cane
I lean upon . . . not plastic switches, knobs
On TV, clock, lamp, radio . . . not locks
On windows, nor the chain I fasten tight
Across the door at night . . .
                              Nothing I touch
Touches me back with pat, hug, kiss, caress,
With quick embrace, spontaneous and warm . . .

I wish . . . I wish someone would fling an arm
Around my shoulders, leave it there awhile,
Careless and kind, till I reach up and press
A hand — a hand that pulses, presses back . . . . .

VALENTINE CLOWN

For Jennifer Coen

Jennifer sends me a Valentine clown —
Insouciant, here he stands,
Offering love to a careless world,
A heart in his outstretched hands.

Jennifer sends me a Valentine clown —
A jaunty cap on his head,
His ruff pure white, his suit sky blue,
But the heart in his hands blood red.

Jennifer sends me a Valentine clown —
Valiant, he hides his fears.
A painted smile on a painted face
Covers the trace of tears.

Jennifer sends me a Valentine clown —
Vulnerable, brave he stands,
Offers his love again and again,
A wounded heart in his hands.

OF THE HOME

"BEDROOM AT ARLES"

Everyone knows you were insane, Van Gogh.
Quite lunatic, yet sane enough to know
The antediluvian truth old Noah knew —
In this mad world all things go two by two —

And so arranged and painted them that way:
Two open windows letting in the day,
Two pillows on the bed, two yellow chairs,
Even the pictures hung in fecund pairs . . .

Yet no one there sets chair straight to the wall,
Or plumps the pillows up, no one at all,
And though the spread is passionately red,
No one waits there, impatient on the bed.

Small wonder, lone Van Gogh, you came undone
When of all your furious works, we bought but one.

WOMEN MY HUSBAND MARRIED

"How Much Am I Bid?"

My husband has married a number of interesting women — including me. His marriage to me was the first in which I saw him participate, and he did a creditable job, in spite of the auction.

Four hundred invitations had gone out for the usual rented top-hat, white-satin, four-o'clock affair, but even I was surprised by the size of the crowd milling around outside the church.

"Heavens," I told my oldest brother, "we'll have to pick up more icecream on the way home!" Then through my Juliet veil I dimly saw on the lawn of the house next door a tattered red flag and the bold, black letters of a sign: **AUCTION TODAY 3 P.M.** I thought of Mother's long lists with their dozens of little check marks. She'd followed Emily Post to the letter. Emily should add another letter: Check church neighborhood for auctions.

It was late June, and far too hot to close the church windows on the pew-jammed friends inside. Even with the windows closed, the competition would have been uneven. The auctioneer had an hour's head start and was nearing the peak of his performance. Our man had just come from a funeral. He wasn't even warmed up.

Nevertheless, he began bravely, opening his black *Ritual* with slow dignity and speaking in the muted tones befitting a solemn occasion.

"Dearly Beloved, we are gathered together here . . . to join this man and this woman — "

"How much am I bid?" boomed the auctioneer. "Who'll start 'er off?"

The minister gave no sign, but his voice was a little less muted. ". . . which is an honorable estate —"

"Estate of a late millionaire!" cried the auctioneer. "The gen-u-wine article! See here — not a sign o' writin' on 'er bottom!"

I felt the bridegroom stir beside me. Not for nothing had he driven me up and down the hills of Maine to at least a dozen country auctions. He knew as well as I that dishes with no signature are often older and more valuable. But could this 'gen-u-wine article' possibly be the one thing we'd been searching for? Could it possibly be the ironstone soup tureen I needed to complete my grandmother's set?

". . . speak now, or else forever hold his peace!" said the minister with authority.

". . . piece o' gen-u-wine ironstone!" said the auctioneer with even more. Then it was ironstone! It had to be a soup tureen!

". . . for better, for worse — " The minister's voice was considerably louder than when he'd started, but he was not and never would be a match for the auctioneer. Ministers are trained in cloistered seminaries to the sound of murmured prayer. The auctioneer had obviously been born on a midway and barked since birth.

". . . for richer, for —"

"Four I hear! Who'll say five?"

"I will," said the groom firmly. I looked at my Britisher in surprise, but he was only promising to forsake all others and cleave himself unto me forever. I felt the wedding ring slip over my finger. *Must be nearly over,* I thought. *Maybe we can get in on the tail end of the bidding.* But I had forgotten the soprano. She entered the fray with a will, throwing in all two hundred pounds on the side of righteousness and valor.

"Oh, promise me that someday you and I-I-I-"

"High?" sang the auctioneer. "Eight ain't high for an old piece like this. Not a chip! Not a crack! Not a sign o' writin' on 'er! Eight I hear! Who'll say nine?"

It took all my willpower to keep quiet. Naturally I was interested in my own wedding, but ironstone soup tureens are really scarce.

". . . now pronounce that they are man and wife." The minister snapped his little book shut considerably faster than he'd opened it and gave one last injunction: "Whom God hath joined, let not man —" and for the first time he allowed himself a glance toward the open window, "put asunder."

"Ten-fifty once! Ten-fifty twice! —"

I was soundly kissed there at the altar — a kiss long enough to twitter the unmarried maidens a bit, but not long enough to make the matrons start pleating their handkerchiefs. My husband, as I said before, did a creditable job at the first wedding in which I saw him participate. It was certainly not his fault that above the sacred hush of our nuptial embrace there floated, with an awful note of finality, the triumphant cry of the auctioneer:

"Sold — to the highest bidder!"

Mendelssohn was never marched to any faster. We tore out of

that Methodist church faster than John Wesley fled the women of Georgia. The car was waiting on the right, but my wonderful new husband knew the way I wanted to go. He pulled me to the left, fumbling in his swallow-tails for bills. At the auctioneer's table the lady with the 'gen-u-wine article' was pocketing her change.

"Madam," my husband bowed in his best ministerial, British, David-Niven manner, "may I present — my wife? We heard inside the valiant battle you waged, and we congratulate you on your victory, but — " and he waved green bills closer and closer to her suspicious face — "we would so much like this — this lovely old piece, for our new home —"

"Hear! Hear!" shouted the crowd. "Let 'em have it! Let 'em have it!"

"Dear lady, for my bride? As a souvenir of the occasion?"

The dear lady hung onto her prize with both perspiring hands until she had fully comprehended the numbers on the bills. Then she let go the dish, my husband let go the cash, and we ran to the waiting car with the cheers of the crowd in our ears.

"Well," grinned my oldest brother, pushing back his top hat and pushing in the clutch, "guess we finally got the old antique auctioned off. How much did that thing cost you, Rev?"

"Too much," said my husband, "but I couldn't have her go through life wishing she'd gone to the auction instead of the wedding. Besides —" he turned the dish upside down — "I sort of wanted to find out for myself."

"Find out what, dear?" I was foolish enough to ask.

"Why —" he put the dish on the floor and his arms around me — "if there's any sign o' writin' on 'er bottom."

It was a huge ironstone platter, not a soup tureen, that the young Reverend and Mrs. Jack Grenfell carried away from the First Methodist Church in Bangor, Maine, that hot June day, and holiday turkeys were served from it for many, many years. For this marriage, perhaps because of its business-like beginning, proved to be a going concern. A few chips, of course. A nick or two here and there. But no cracks. No breaks. The gen-u-wine article in every way.

WHEN THEY WERE SMALL

Pamela
Oh, the joy of Pam, aged two,
Finding where blueberries grew
Low on bushes, close to shore —
*   "More cherries, Mommy! Pam pick more!"*

Small hands reaching, brown eyes keen,
Distinguishing the blue from green,
First sweet taste of Nature's store —
*   "More cherries, Mommy! Pam pick more!"*

Nana's Camp
Long Pond, Maine, 1950

John Millard
My little boy is going on four
Isn't a baby anymore
Slams in and out and bangs the door
And 'asking permission' is a bore —
Now he's most four!

The baby smile now is a real boy's grin
With a gleam in the eye of original sin
And the noise he makes an unholy din
As he runs on the lawn where the grass has been —
Now he's most four!

But sometimes, still, there's a special joy
When he forgets he's a great big boy
Lays his head on his mother's knee
As he used to do when he was three
Lets himself be loved one minute more . . .
Then off again with a shout and a roar
To the Grown-up Land, the Big Boy Land

of Four.

Bethel, Connecticut, 1945

Lornagrace
Only been six for a little while
Innocent eyes that know no guile
Sweet lips curved in a shy half-smile
  My flower girl . . . down the aisle

Floats in organdy, three yards wide
Pink taffeta on the underside
Scattering roses for the bride
  My flower girl . . . down the aisle

Little finger cocked high in the air
Drops each petal with a flair
*As if to say, **"Bride, step right there!"***
  My flower girl . . . down the aisle

Whispers a secret with high glee:
"I'll be in two weddings, Daddy, see?
This one for Ginny, another for me!"
  My flower girl . . . down the aisle

Bayside, New York, 1950

LEAVING THE PARSONAGE

The van has left. Pale sunbeams pierce the gloom
Of thick-leafed maples and the one pine tree.
Walk once more through each strangely tidy room,
Clicking the shutter of dear memory.

Five Christmases we had the tree just there . . .
How well the plants did on that window sill . . .
Jill helped me paint this old red rocking chair . . .
My sister's hands are idle now, and still . . .

***"Let's have a service,"** John would always say,*
Lighting the taper with elaborate care . . .
***"Pass out the hymnals —"** See the hallowed play*
Of candlelight on small heads bowed in prayer . . .

*God bless who comes . . . **"Yes, dear, a minute more —"***
God bless who leaves . . . walk softly . . . close the door.

LLOYDIE

Lloydie was different when he came home from the war —
Remote, somehow, as though he'd seen and done
Unfamiliar things the family could never know.
He talked not at all. **"What was it like?"** *I asked.*
"What did you do over there for three long years?"
"It was hot. I ran a bulldozer a lot."
"Digging roads? On South Pacific islands?"

"No —"

He turned, walked away, turned back, said two short words:
"Digging graves."

That was all. Today I stand looking down

At his, at red geraniums, lush grass,
Or looking up at wide blue sky piled high
With popcorn clouds, and think of other days . . .

Red cranberries strung with popcorn, hung on trees,
Dancing to Guy Lombardo New Year's Eve,
Fishing, swimming, laughing with a boy
I knew and loved, the brother with whom I grew
Who went to war — and of a silent man,
A strangely different man I never knew.

SIXTIES PARENT

Classes were changing. Dr. Hightower called to me down the crowded school corridor.

"Mrs. G., Mrs. G., wait up! Pamela called —" My principal is a long-distance walker. His great strides brought him quickly nearer. "Said to tell you she found your diamond —" He was beside me now — "in her prayer book!"

"It's been lost six months. She and Eliot should pray oftener."

He grinned. "She said you'd say that. Said to be sure to tell you it was in her *second-best* prayer book."

"Thanks." I hurried to my study hall.

Rev had given me my one-and-only diamond. I'd worn it for a year before we were married, kept it safe for thirty-two. Pamela had had it six years and it had been lost for six months. I'd given it to her the Palm Sunday she and Eliot told us they planned to be married at Pam's Commencement in May. Even in 1969 I was old-fashioned enough to think every engaged girl should have a diamond ring.

Pam herself had been perfectly happy with the little bell ring Eliot had bought for her one day in Harvard Square for five dollars. The parakeet had swung on that one for a year while it hung in the bird cage and Eliot waited for courage and a propitious moment to tell his parents he was getting married half-way through college. Now I was going to take my ring back. Pamela could just wait till I was dead to have it.

She'd been sweet to call, though. I glanced at the study hall clock — yes, daytime rates, even in California. She knew I'd been worried about the ring. Second-best prayer book, indeed! Nothing second-best about Pamela, though. She was first-rate all the way.

"What's your name, Pam?" the kids in kindergarten used to ask her.

"Pamela Margaret P. Peggy Pushaw Gulliver Pomroy Coffin

Grenfell," she'd answer in one breath. How they'd laugh and clap and ask her again.

"What's your name, Pam? Tell us again!"

"Pamela Margaret P. Peggy —" It was my great-grandmother's name, with all the generations in between added on. Pamela was proud of her name. Names meant something to her — names and words.

Long before she could read or write, she'd come stand by my desk and dictate 'poems' for me to type. The school teacher in me was strong. As she dictated, I'd sometimes suggest a different word. It was always refused, but sometimes I'd type it in anyway.

"Read it back," she'd say at last. Brown eyes glowing, expectant, she'd listen to her poem — sometimes a full page — until I came to my word.

"All right!" she'd shout, eyes flashing fire, brown curls bobbing in rage. "Leave it that way! And sign it Clarine Coffin Grenfell!" Several days would pass before I'd again have the privilege of typing a 'poem.'

Her own word. Her own way. Yes, Pamela would fight for that to her last breath, to the last ounce of her strength. Her own truth. Her own justice.

She had, when she was seven, one live dog, a brindle boxer named Rebellion, and 127 other dogs — metal, stuffed, wooden, plastic. They crowded the shelves in her room and competed with the nine breeds of dogs romping around the wallpaper in the canine pattern Pam had picked out for herself. Most of the 127 were healthy, but one, a two-inch metal collie, had fallen from his shelf and broken his leg. It lay beside him on a wad-of-white-cotton hospital bed, awaiting the proper glue. Each day when she came from school, Pamela went straight to her room to see how her dog was doing. One winter afternoon she came flying back downstairs — Ollie had been there, dusted bookshelves. Her dog, her poor, sick, hurt dog, was gone! Only his leg was left, tucked way in the corner! Call Ollie! Call her at once!

"She thought it was trash." I hung up the phone. "She threw it out." Fury. Unbelievable. Mad dash for five garbage cans lined up in the snow outside. Tip them over. Upside down. Coffee grounds. Egg shells. Onion peelings.

"Pamela, wait! I'll spread newspapers —" Paw, paw, paw, on hands and knees. Bring flashlights. Paw again. The third time through, long after dark, we found the tiny dog buried in the ashes from the fireplace. Brought him in, scrubbed him clean, put him and his leg together again on a fresh wad of cotton. Only then did Pamela scrub her own sooty self, eat her cold supper, go to bed.

Next day her father brought home metal glue.

She never trusted Ollie after that. On cleaning days, once a week, Pam had all the invisible illnesses — headache, earache, toothache, stomach ache. I'd leave notes: "Pamela is home sick today. Please give her soup for lunch. See that she stays in bed."

Ollie never saw the notes. And Pam did not stay in bed. She stayed under it. Even as Ollie walked up the long drive from the bus stop, Pamela would be grabbing the note, the peanut butter jar, crackers, jelly and a spoon if she had time, and making a mad dash for her room. There, scrouged in the farthest corner behind the bed ruffle, she read, protected her four-hour food supply from hasty swipes of the dry mop, and kept an eye on her 127 dogs while Ollie cleaned the upstairs. Once she forgot and gave herself away. "Mama, why does Ollie keep saying 'damn, damn, damn' all the while she's cleaning *my* room — she doesn't in the others?"

1963 was a hard autumn for fourteen-year-old girls. In September, when four children almost her age were killed in a Sunday School in Birmingham, Pamela wept. She'd been in Sunday School herself that morning and could not believe such a thing had happened. She waited for the newscast to be repeated and, when it was, hated the announcer — "Damn his objective voice!" — and wept again, and wrote a poem.

Two months later Pamela was in school when the word flashed through — the President, shot, dying, dead. JFK. Her President. Once again she could not believe. Could not believe the world could be that bad.

"Why do we have to cancel the Pep Rally? We play Conard tomorrow —" she heard a cheerleader complain — and lashed out at her. Went to the library, put her head down, and after awhile asked Mrs. DeGroat if she could use the typewriter, and wrote a poem.

And on Saturday another . . . on Sunday another . . . on Monday another. She sent *Four Days in Sequence* to Hyannis and to the White House after it was published, and Rose and Jacqueline both wrote to thank her, but Pamela's faith in her country had been badly shaken.

Still, she could not *not* believe in America. So she campaigned for McCarthy. Slept with nine other girls on a dirt floor in New Hampshire before the February primary. Had no blanket — only a plastic sleeping bag. Could not sleep. Cried quietly, so as not to waken the others. Remembered her heavy cape upstairs, crept up and got it, wrapped herself in it, flung herself down — and woke everyone with her screams. She's forgotten the deep pockets were stuffed full of big McCarthy buttons, all with long sharp pins.

But he won. And Johnson quit. So maybe a few boys are alive today because of Pamela and college kids and cellars in New Hampshire.

At Hall High School in West Hartford, she played Rheba in *You Can't Take It with You* because, of course, there were no black girls at Hall High and none of the other white girls wanted to put on that messy black makeup. So Pam played Rheba and brought down the house when she smashed those plates — "Damn it, Donald!"

She brought down the whole school when she campaigned for Student Council — sang her campaign speech before a thousand kids, strumming the guitar she'd acquired with eleven books of *S and H Green Stamps* after a Peter, Paul and Mary concert at the Bushnell. The big issue that year was a smoking lounge for students.

"Cigarettes will ruin your life," Pam strummed soulfully, *"spoil your teeth and kill your ba-bee . . ."* Landslide vote for Pamela Grenfell, secretary of Student Council. A week later she resigned. Her father had been transferred from Hartford to Darien. Pamela left the gifted students' program she'd been in since third grade, left the much-loved friends she'd traveled through school with for eight happy, productive years, moved to Darien.

White ghetto. Ninety-eight per cent WASP. The town Laura Hobson had in mind when she wrote *Gentleman's Agreement*. Darien High School for her junior year.

The first day of school Pamela carried her lunch tray to five different tables in the cafeteria, each with empty chairs. "You can't sit here," the girls chanted, or "We're saving these for our friends," or "These seats are taken." She went to the garbage window, dumped her tray, never went into the cafeteria again. "I hate Darien," she said. "I'm not staying here. I'm going to college in '65, not '66 . Can't I, Daddy? I'll be sixteen!"

So she took her college boards, applied to Mount Holyoke, where her sister was a junior — "Fun for Lorni and me to have one year of college together!" — and when her counselor called her to his office in March and said, "You have to be thinking about senior year, Pam, college, achievement tests —" Pam said, "I've already taken them, already been accepted, with scholarship —" and his teeth fell out. Because no one at Darien High had ever done that before, and Pam's English teacher had given her a *B-* because, he said, she didn't write very well. But a year later in South Hadley when her parents opened the white Commencement program to see their older daughter's name, there was their younger daughter's name, too — *Sproule Prize for the freshman who shows the most promise of a gift for writing, awarded to Pamela Margaret Grenfell, '69.*

October, 1967. We were watching the six o'clock news in Darien. The First Peace Moratorium. Hundreds of college kids milling around the Pentagon, protesting the draft, the Vietnam War, sleeping on the ground around bonfires, trying to 'storm' the building, destroy draft records.

"Isn't that Pamela?" our older daughter asked suddenly.

"Pamela!" I said stupidly. "Where?"

"Going up the steps — the one with the biggest placard — oh, she's gone!" I dialed the college. Person-to-person for Miss Pamela Grenfell.

"No, Pamela isn't here."

"Can you tell me where she is? Where she's signed out for?" Long wait.

"Pamela is spending the weekend with friends." She certainly was — Eldridge Cleaver, Norman Mailer, Alan Ginsberg, and one enemy, President Johnson. We waited for the 11 o'clock news. Yes, it was Pam, the one with the biggest placard.

Sunday night when students from Smith, Amherst, Harvard, Holyoke went to board their chartered bus to take them back for classes — no Monday morning cuts allowed in 1967 — they found it tipped over on its side, smashed. No one had any money left for other transportation. What to do . . . Then Eliot remembered he had an aunt whose husband worked at the Pentagon, a nuclear submarine consulting engineer. Maybe she would . . . she did. Lend money to fly to Bradley Field. America. Pamela. Like all young people, she hated war, hurt, fighting, killing.

So she did the things she knew how to do for peace. She broadcast her religion — ran *Sister Pammie's Gospel Hour* — *"A little more Jesus Christ, a little less rock 'n roll"* — on the college radio station for two years, and got made manager, and people listened to her because she was for real. She went to Yale and Wesleyan and read her poems. One April she got a thousand people to celebrate *Gentle Thursday* with flowers, balloons, and fun. Mrs. Gettell came, enjoyed herself, wrote Pam a note thanking her for 'making Mount Holyoke a better place to live.' And until she read about Pamela Grenfell's Gentle Thursday Celebration in the College Issue of *Mademoiselle* the next fall, the wife of the president of the college didn't even know that she herself had been a flower child and a hippie for one whole lovely spring day. By then Pamela was in love.

"His name is Eliot," she told us. "One *l*, as in T.S. His mother's an English major." Eliot's thick, brown hair was very long when she brought him home at Christmas. So long it flipped up, all around. His jeans were not quite so faded as Pam's. He was very quiet, barely spoke a word. They came on the afternoon of the first Parsonage Open House in our new church in Westchester County. All afternoon they sat in their faded jeans on the floor in front of the fireplace, clutching each other, as some two-hundred new parishioners and the district superintendent streamed through.

"This is my daughter Pamela from Mount Holyoke and her friend, Mr. Smith from Harvard . . ." After everyone had gone, I suggested *Scrabble*. I had to find out what was underneath all that hair. Pamela said she was tired, going to bed, but Eliot said he'd play one game.

I am a very good Scrabble player. I played hard. My very best. Eliot made eight-letter words. Several times. He beat me by 336 points. I hated him. I loved him. I went upstairs and shook Pamela's shoulder.

"Marry him. Someday he'll get a haircut."

She would not send out the 500+ wedding invitations as her brother had done in '65, her sister in '66. "I only want the people I love. I'll write little notes." She did. To her third-grade teacher, her Hall High principal. To the people she'd known in her father's churches that she considered Christians. Almost everybody she invited came.

"No processional, Daddy. Nothing fancy. We'll just be there. When the right moment comes, you can marry us."

When she'd first gone to college, she'd looked through the Yellow Pages, found the nearest Methodist church some miles from campus. "Yes," the minister had told her, "someone will be glad to pick you up." The 'someone' turned out to be Dr. John Piper of the MHC Department of Religion. Pamela had gone back and forth to church with him, his wife and children, had taught a Sunday School class for emotionally disturbed children, been on the administrative board. Now Dr. Piper helped her father marry her in the college chapel.

"No expensive dress," Pam said. "I don't want you worried about money, Mother. Make me one." So she'd found a few yards of raw silk in some rag shop on Harvard Square and I had made her dress. Embroidered her Juliet cap with tiny seed pearls from a necklace that had belonged to her Grandmother Grenfell. She was a radiant bride. She was Pam.

No rented Tuxedo for Eliot. Nothing phony. He wore his brown jacket. It was a handsome jacket. We sang *Joyful, Joyful* and *All Creatures of Our God and King*. Pamela's brother gave her away. Her sister and her brother's wife were her maids. She carried lilies-of-the-valley because they are her father's favorite flower and because she was the last child to leave home. Friends came from Cambridge and, at the reception, lit incense sticks, waved them under the noses of the third-grade teacher and the high school principal.

She got married one day and got her degree the next. With white tissue paper wound round her arm in silent Vietnam protest. And moved from MHC to Harvard and had the piano in the kitchen and made souffles while Eliot played sonatas and got his B.A. and his Ph.D. and they both produced Miranda and moved to California and never came home to live again at all.

My daughter, Pamela. Mine on lease for sixteen short years. While she grew up. While she taught me many things. About words. And integrity. And compassion. About being honest.

A bell sounded. The study hall was over. Pamela could keep the diamond ring her father had given me. God bless it, and her, and Eliot, their child . . . and both their prayer books.

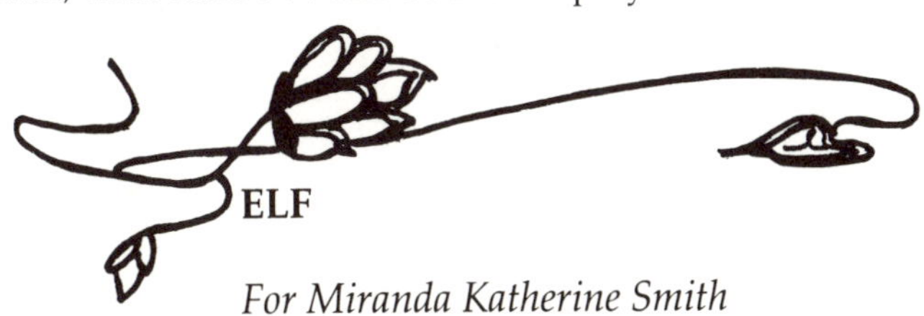

ELF

For Miranda Katherine Smith

Miranda is a fairy, a leprechaun, a sprite,
A tiny Cornish pesky with a wide, wide smile!
She dances like a moonbeam, a butterfly, an elf,
And all the while her laughing eyes beguile!

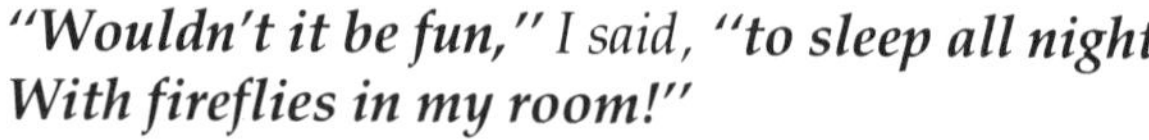

LU-MIN-ES-CENT NIGHT

For James Edgar Bowron III

"Wouldn't it be fun," I said, *"to sleep all night*
With fireflies in my room!"
                              Gram looked at me.
"In Maine we call them lightning bugs," she said.
"Can I have a jar?"
                    "Punch holes in the lid for air."

So I chased them round the lawn, caught five, then ten,
Set the jar beside my bed, turned out the light . . .

They tried to fly, climbed up the sides, fell down,
Crawled around, tried again, fell down, their orange lights
Going on and off . . . Gram came and stood in the door.
"Lu-min-es-cent," she said at last. **"May as well learn the**
          word . . .
They make their light, you know, in their own little tails —
Lu-min-es-cent . . . **Well, goodnight. Don't forget your**
          prayers."

I closed my eyes, opened them. They were still climbing up,
Falling down, climbing up, the lights in their tails going off
And on and off . . . I squeezed my eyes tight shut . . .
Opened them, climb up, fall down, crawl around, on and off . . .
I went at last to Grandma's room.
                              "Grandma —
We have to let them go."
                    "Yes, I thought you might."
So together we went barefoot to the farthest edge
Of the lawn, unscrewed the lid, watched them fly up, up
Toward the big unblinking stars, their orange lights
Going on and off and on . . . .
"I don't suppose," Gram said, **"you remember the word."**
"No, I don't. 'Course not," I said and ran to my bed
Over dew wet grass that lu-min-es-cent night.

EMPTY PLACES

When I glance at the lake on a summer day and see
Far out, bobbing on the waves, an empty boat —
No shock of blond hair glinting in the sun,
No strong, tanned shoulders straining at the oars —
I do not panic, call life guards . . . I know
If I look through glasses, focus carefully,
I'll see, dangling over the side, a young boy hand,
Thin fingers dribbling water now and then,
As Jeb, stretched flat in the bottom, gazes up
Hour after hour into endless blue Maine sky,
Giving Someone up there ample time and space
To fill with shining visions, endless dreams
The empty places in a young boy heart.

HEROES FROM CAMP WINDOWS

For St. John Grenfell Bowron

Small boy has struggled, climbed the highest rock,
Surveys from eight feet up, the whole wide world —
Lake, forest, mountain . . . but what's this? Has he
Like many an older conqueror been caught short?
Unbuckling belt, he casts a covert glance
Toward windows, turns a modest back, drops shorts,
And waters manfully, feet wide apart,
Wild fern and columbine.

                 Quite sure he'll be
Someday a Ph.D., I superimpose
On drooping small white drawers a long black gown,
Top it with velvet hood, and, smiling, spread
Great dollops of red jelly on his bread.

GODDAUGHTER, GRANDDAUGHTER

For Clara Beatrice Bowron

Clara Beatrice Bowron, 10,
of Kansas City, MO,
. . . gets up at 5 a.m. to watch the confluence of the planets
. . . feeds her dog Barkis, eats her egg-on-toast, arrives at
prestigious Sunset Hill School for Girls at 8
. . . goes to six classes, gets five A's, and one B +
. . . takes part in a gymnastics show where she excels in
>*knee bends*
>*head stands*
>*balance beam*
. . . comes home at 3, curls her beautiful blonde hair on her
mother's electric curling iron without burning either neck or
fingers
. . . walks briskly to Central United Methodist for
>*acolyte practice at 4*
>*choir practice at 5*
>*church supper at 6*
>*a musical play, **The Babble of Babel,** at 7,*
>*in which she, of course, has the lead and so*
. . . bows graciously when presented a long-stemmed American
Beauty rose from one of her many male admirers
. . . arrives home at 9, full of vim, vigor, and vitality, asking only
"What's to eat?"
. . . lays out clothes for the morrow, says prayers, goes to sleep.

Clara Beatrice Bowron, 10,
of Kansas City, MO,
goddaughter, granddaughter
is quite a girl.

I asked her once, when we were having a picnic on the White House
>*lawn, **"Would you like to live here?"***
*"Oh," she replied nonchalantly, **"I suppose I might be***
>***President someday."***

VIOLETS FOR MY MAMA

For Trelawney Jean Grenfell

When I was a little girl like you,
Five or four or three or two,
One thing in spring I'd always do —
Pick violets for my Mama!

I'd wait for the snow to melt away
Through March and April till early May
When suddenly, near Mother's Day,
There'd be violets for my Mama!

I'd run to pick the bits of sky
Fallen in patches far and nigh,
Wondering why they made her cry,
These violets picked for Mama.

She'd hold them in her hands quite still
While I filled a cup for the window sill,
And always hidden tears would spill
On violets picked for Mama!

But now I know . . . she remembered, too —
Because it's a thing all little girls do —
Once she'd been a child, like me, like you,
Picking violets for her Mama!

So, Lawni, look — are the fields still bare?
Has the blue sky fallen anywhere?
Run quick to pick! Kneel . . . say a prayer
For violets and for Mamas!

*Reprinted from **Lantern***

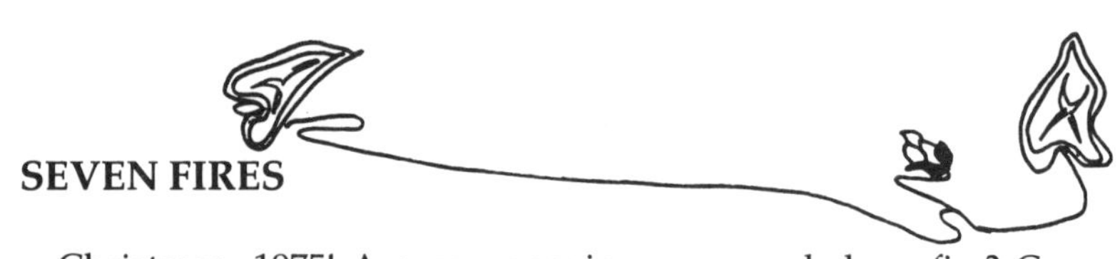

SEVEN FIRES

Christmas, 1975! Are you opening your cards by a fire? Come share the warmth and joy of ours — seven fireplaces now where we feel very much at home! Stretch out your hands across the miles . . .

"IS NOT MY WORD LIKE AS A FIRE?" *Jeremiah 23:29*

In Westport, Connecticut, Clarine still spends her days with words — her twelfth year as reading consultant there. Almost always her landlady, Margaret Flint, who once taught English at University of Kansas, has a fire burning, a cup of tea brewing, and shares Clarine's small satisfactions — a boy she tutors has raised his SAT scores from 510 to 680, a doctor who read 200 wpm now speed-reads 2000, the school magazine she advised has won a Medalist rating from Columbia. But come Friday afternoon, it's hurry 75 miles up the Merritt Parkway to . . .

"BEHOLD THE FIRE AND THE WOOD . . ." *Genesis 22:7*

612 Fern Street, West Hartford, where the Grenfells are celebrating their 11th Christmas — 1956-64, 1973-75. Here the logs crackling on the hearth are from their own apple, dogwood, oak, or pine. Here old friends, as well as new, know the way. Jack enjoys his third year of early retirement, teaches Bible Class for Bill Carroll in West Hartford's exciting United Methodist Church, raises roses and tomatoes, works hard as charter member and president of a 450-member AARP, baptizes grandchildren . . .

"AS SOON AS THEY WERE COME TO LAND,
THEY SAW A FIRE OF COALS . . ." *John 21:9*

Yes, Miranda Katherine Smith's fireplace is a fire of coals, a barbecue grill on a patio in Southern California. Miranda (from *The Tempest*, of course) is a precocious, wide-eyed darling who chose her dad's birthdate for her own, February 4. Her christening party at Harvard Epworth UMC was a happy affair for some sixty 'friends and relations' and soon after, Eliot's Harvard doctorate completed, the Smiths moved to Riverside.

Here Pamela marvels at and mothers Miranda, conducts children's tours at Riverside Museum, works for an MBA, while Eliot plays tennis and teaches psychology at University of California. The Smiths, Methodists for six years in Cambridge, are giving Eliot's denomination a turn and worshiping at St. George Episcopal Church. We Easterners miss you, yes, we even miss Fred, the Dog.

"WHILE I WAS MUSING, THE FIRE BURNED." *Psalm 39:3*

Musing by the fire in Bangor, Maine, Clara Beatrice Coffin celebrates her 91st birthday. Yes, Lloyd and Margie gave her a party at her old home, 782 Broadway, with twenty lively friends attending. Yes, she still scolds Clarine for spoiling her children, still corrects her enunciation. "Say po-ta-to, dear!" And though there is constant pain now, there is also constant fortitude. God bless your 92nd Christmas, our brilliant, spunky, independent Maine mother. Please aim for your 100th!

"WHERE NO WOOD IS, THE FIRE GOETH OUT . . ."
Proverbs 26:20

No lack of wood on the Bowron land in Baltimore, Maryland, and no lack of small hands to gather kindling, especially if hot buttered popcorn is the incentive! Jeb (7) are you really old enough to be an altar boy? Can Clara (4) really embroider pillows? Can anyone resist the cherubic smile of St. John (2)?

The Bowrons, too, are a church-oriented family. Peter is vestryman and lay leader and Lorna a church-school teacher at St. John's Episcopal. Last year the Bowrons directed a tour of British castles and this spring will explore museums and such in Belgium. These tours are sponsored by the Walters Gallery, where Peter is curator of 18th century baroque art. Lucky Bowrons!

"WHO MAKETH . . . HIS MINISTERS A FLAME OF FIRE."
Hebrews 1:7

In the Methodist Manse at Guilford, Maine, the glass-enclosed fire draws like a magnet. Here we celebrated Thanksgiving. The little girls with the Cornish names — Tamarleigh (4), Tallessyn and Trelawney (1) gave us joy. Linda, more beautiful each year, fed our bodies with pies made from her own pumpkins, blueberries picked on Carrying Place Island. John Millard fed our spirits with his Loyalty Day Service.

We were, indeed, much moved by the seriousness and dedication of the church members as they laid their pledges, up a triumphant 75%, on the altar. No doubt Guilford will continue to be one of Maine's largest and strongest Methodist churches, a spiritual powerhouse. The minister's parents received the same warm welcome as in Summerfield, NYC, John's last pastorate. As always, we thanked God for the affection that surrounds the minister's family.

Opening an old anniversary booklet on John's desk, we saw a picture of the Reverend Albert E. Morris, once superintendent of the Guilford church and the first minister I remember as pastor of First Methodist, Bangor, where I started Sunday School sixty years ago. The Guilford church . . . Reverend Morris . . . me, a child of four . . . our beloved son . . . the Guilford church. So Christian love goes round in circles, "returning after many days." Pray for the Guilford Church during this first year of John's ministry, and you Bangor Coffins who have worshiped here already — keep coming back.

> "I SAW AS IT WERE A SEA OF GLASS, MINGLED WITH FIRE . . . AND THEM THAT HAD GOTTEN THE VICTORY . . . STAND ON THE SEA OF GLASS, HAVING THE HARPS OF GOD, AND THEY SING . . ." *Revelation 15:2,3*

At Alamoosook Lake in Orland, Maine, the fieldstone fireplace stands ten feet high. Red sunsets in our sea of glass reflect the flames from giant logs. Here each year God helps us 'put it all together.' Here we (fifteen of us now — father, mother, six children, seven grandchildren) gather around the piano . . . on the shore of the lake . . . by the fire to sing . . .

> " . . . THE SONG OF THE LAMB SAYING
> GREAT AND MARVELOUS ARE THY WORKS
> LORD GOD ALMIGHTY!
> JUST AND TRUE ARE THY WAYS,
> THOU KING OF SAINTS!
> WHO SHALL NOT FEAR THEE, O LORD, AND GLORIFY
> THY NAME?
> FOR THOU ONLY ART HOLY,
> FOR ALL NATIONS SHALL COME AND WORSHIP BEFORE
> THEE." *Revelation 15:3,4*

Sing with us this Christmas the Song of the Lamb! Glorify the Name! Come and worship!

Merry Christmas!

Jack and Clarine Grenfell

ALWAYS THE SOMETHING ELSE

These raw March days — trees leafless, frozen ruts
Scarring the barren earth, no singing birds —
I remember how you used to long for spring.

Coming in cold, dragging the heavy bags,
*You'd sigh and say, **"I wish the spring would come!"***
And later when white crocuses pushed up
And daffodils and pale blue hyacinths,
*You'd stand by the kitchen door: **"I think I'll take***
A little ride out in the country, dear —"
*Wanting me to answer, **"Wait! I'm coming, too!"***

Why didn't I? . . . Willows were hanging pale . . .
The hedges sunny with forsythia . . . buds
On the maple trees exploding red . . . why?

Always the something else — the bills to pay,
Letters to write, the cleaning, phoning, meals . . .
No time for looking, dreaming, holding hands . . .
In spite of Housman's poem, no time for spring
And blossoming cherry trees . . . no time for love.

Oh, I'll plant pansies by your stone, come May.
Small velvet faces will look up at me
Reproachfully, for spring will always come —

But never again for you, my dearest dear . . .
And never again with you . . . . never with you.

*Reprinted from **Trinity Tidings***

SET OUT THE CUPS

When I get home, I thought, I'll make the tea.
I'll put the kettle on, set out the cups —
Yours white, mine blue — and then we'll sit and talk
About the service . . .

How the people sang

The 'Alleluias' in your favorite hymn!
How blue the heather was — almost as blue
As that you picked in Cornwall long ago
And tucked into my hair! And how our son,
So like you, made them laugh (Imagine that!)
With loving stories of his dad, and how
The gentle scent of roses followed us
As we filed out to stand among the stones . . .

When I get home, when I get home, I thought,
I'll make the tea, we'll sit for hours and chat.
I'll put the kettle on, set out the cups —
Set out the cups . . .

no, put the white one back.

'THE STUFF THEY SELL'

*Today they put the **FOR SALE** sign on the lawn —*
Came early, pounded in the pointed stakes,
And left without a word.
                              I watched through a blur
*Of sudden, unexpected tears . . . **FOR SALE***
*Was it old Khayyam wondered **'what they buy***
One-half so precious as the stuff they sell'?

'The stuff they sell —'
                              White lilacs bending low
Along the hedge, red tulips trumpeting . . .
In May around the bird bath, violets
That two small girls knelt patiently to pick
Each Mother's Day . . . pink petals fluttering down
From apple, dogwood, pear tree all in bloom . . .
One shy, brown cottontail we called Bryl Creme . . .
The mourning doves' complaint, my cardinal,
A flash of red against the giant pine
Where Rebel lay, head down, disconsolate,
September days when all trooped off to school . . .

***'The stuff they sell'** —*
                              Twin lions standing guard,
Stout British sentinels . . . inside the door
***"The house still smells the same!"** the children say*
On brief, infrequent visits from away . . .
Children with children now, amazed to find
The half-forgotten smell of home unchanged —
Pizza and chocolate chips, warm redolence
Of turkey stuffed with Bell's . . . Pam's yellow bread,
Great fragrant loaves of saffron, baked for Dad . . .
The Easter lily Doran's always sent,
Pungent and piercing sweet . . . the bearskin rug
Before the fire, burnt marshmallows, green boughs
From balsam Christmas trees exploding sparks
That shot our Twelfth Night prayers straight up to God . . .

'The stuff they sell —'
Remembered voices, sounds . . .
Laughter and hymns and always poetry
Easing the irksome task . . . blue **Sound and Sense**
Propped open by the sink — **'And hast thou slain**
The Jabberwock?' . . . **'It is morning, Senlin says . . .'**
And **'When, oh, when shall we three meet again. . .'**
Parties to say farewell to comrades, friends,
To teachers, preachers, soldiers, sailors — then
Parties to welcome home again . . . birthdays
With candle-dripping cakes, Hall-Conard kids,
Their blue or crimson jackets wet with snow,
Crashing in droves when Lorni turned sixteen,
The driveway jammed with cars. **"I didn't know**
My daughter had so many friends! I'll go
For Coke!" John's Slingerland, the flying sticks,
The thumping bass — **"Gonna rock around the clock**
Tonight, gonna rock, gonna rock, in my blue suede shoes . . ."
The piano painted pink . . . the rumpus room
Alive with noise . . .
Then four November days
When all, transfixed before the screen, met death . . .
Immobilized and mute, except for Pam
Who crept away between dry sobs to write
Her anguished verse . . .

The rooms all tidy now . . . no wild array
Of dog collection, tutus, ballet shoes,
No skis, no skates, no flying flat white seeds
From Jack o' Lanterns scooped with careless haste . . .
Beneath the warming lamp no wild duck eggs
For science project . . . gerbil, mouse, long gone . . .
No frenzied midnight sewing for the prom,
The play . . . no cardboard angel wings to spray
Bright gold . . .

*   The rooms all tidy now, silent except*
For the lingering sound of pounding echoing still
From hammered stakes sunk deep into the lawn —
The long green sloping lawn where once we raked
Great heaps of scarlet leaves against the wind
*And ran and jumped and shouted Shelley's **Ode** —*
'Yellow, and black, and pale, and hectic red,
***Pestilence-stricken multitudes —'** and raked*
And ran and leaped again and laughed and loved
As if life stayed forever young, unchanged . . .
As if green lawns stayed always fresh and green . . .
As if leaves never fell . . . nor sudden tears . . .
Nor men . . . as if . . . as if . . .

*Today they put the **FOR SALE** sign on the lawn.*

DIVORCE — A LESSON IN VOCABULARY

When I saw the father, body wracked with sobs,
Stand by the window watching the yellow bus
Bring children home from school — but none to him,
Not one, ever again, to run to him,
*Paper held high, **"Daddy! I got a star!"** —*
Then I began to understand the word,
The hurt, the pain, the anguish of the word,
The lonely desolation of the word . . . .

And when I saw his great hands clench, unclench
To strike at futile tears, and clench again,
I came at last to comprehend the word,
The never-ending sorrow of the word,
To know the mordant meaning of the word.

THE LONELY COLD

For Tallessyn Zawn Grenfell

My Tallessyn cried when I said goodbye. Big tears
Filled the beautiful brown eyes, hung tremulous,
Rolled slowly down flushed cheeks. **"Grandma,"** *she sobbed,*
"Why — do you stay here such a little time?"

I looked at her, not quite believing. Who
These many years cares when one comes, or when
One goes? But these were honest tears. They flowed
Straight from the heart of the guileless child to mine,
Warmed it against the lonely cold of old.

I held her close, promised to come back soon —
And will remember always . . . Talli cried.

Reprinted from the **Lantern**

PONY BOY

For Tamarleigh Grace Grenfell

Sometimes in dreams I ride Pony Boy again —
Round and round the track, high up, the wind in my hair . . .
Mommy's there, looking proud, and when we get home, my Dad
Comes bustling in, gives us all big hugs, asks **"How**
Did the lesson go, TG?" *and we all sit down*
Round the table, look up at the blackboard to see whose turn
For the grace, and it's mine, so we all join hands, and I say,
"Thank You, God! Thank You, God! Thank You, God, for my
   family!"
Sometimes in dreams I ride Pony Boy again —
Round the track on his back high up the wind in my hair,
Mommy's there, and Dad, and we all join hands for the
   prayer. . . .

S-T-E-P

For the Reverend Linda Littlefield Grenfell

A dozen Magic Markers lay scattered round the rug
as three small girls colored wedding cards.
"I'm making my cake green,"
Lawni, the artistic one, said,
"'cause my ribbons and flowers and stuff are all green."
Talli reached for the blue.
"Great idea! I'll match mine, too."
"Aunt Betty knows I like pink," said TG.
"That's why she dyed my stuff all pink."
So they made green layer cakes, blue brides, pink grooms
till they came to the words . . .

*"Do we print **MOTHER**," Talli asked, "along with **DAD**?"*
"No, she's not our mother," said TG, the oldest.
*"She's a step. Print step — **S-T-E-P**"*
"What's a STEP?" Lawni asked. "I mean —
what's it mean?"
"You've played it —" TG told her — "on the dock at Alamoo.
It's where you cover your eyes and say
'Take a step — a little bunny hop or a big giant step —'"
"Oh, that," said Lawni. "I knew it was a way
to get from one place to another place."

*So they all printed **S-T-E-P** until TG said,*
"I'm making up words to go with mine.
*I've got **SOMEONE** for the **S**,*
*And **POETRY** for the **P**."*
"She sure knows poems, same as Dad," Lawni said.
"Knows yards and yards by heart."
"Said funny ones in the car," said Talli.
"Even Dad was laughing — Did you notice, TG?"
*"Sure — I'll put **ENJOY** for the **E** —*
*I'm done! Want to hear? **S-T-E-P** —*
SOMEONE
TO
ENJOY
POETRY with!"*

"That's good," said Lawni. "Will you help me?
She likes to ski and swim, but those are S,
*and she likes to **BIKE**, but that's a **B**."*
*"How about **PIZZA**? She ate a big piece*
when we stopped on the way?"
*"**PIECE** o' **PIZZA** — That's two.*
Thanks, Talli. What's yours?"
*"I got **PEOPLE** and **PARTIES** 'cause she says we can come*
on all our vacations, 'n I bet we'll have
***PARTIES** and **PICNICS** 'n all kinds of fun —"*
*"There's **PREACH** 'n **PRAY** —*
She's a minister," said TG,
who may be one herself someday . . . .

So they colored wedding cards, gave them happily
*to the **WONDERFUL NEW STEP**, who was*
    SOMEONE
    TO
    ENJOY
    ***PICNICS, PARTIES, PEOPLE, PIZZA, POEMS** with and*
    SOMEONE
    TO
    ESPECIALLY
    PRAY FOR
On a June wedding day
When three small girls in dainty white dresses
    with blue-green-pink sashes and
    pink-green-blue hairbows
Carried dainty bouquets of green-pink-blue daisies
    down a wide church aisle
To gaze trustingly up at a beautiful bride
Who would help a broken family take
    ***BIG GIANT STEPS** to get*
    from one place to another — from alone to together —
    from silence to laughter — from sadness to 'lived-happily-
    forever-and-ever-after!'

MATHEMATICS

Lonely as I could not be, my love,
Had I your sweet completion never known;
Lonely as white pen is lone above
Deserted sea whence her loved cob has flown.

The ship yearns not for harbor never seen,
Nor lowlander for mountain height unscaled.
The sunless cavern, missing not the sheen
Of light on waves, joys in its shadows veiled.

But I, my love, have known your arms at night,
Have heard your heartbeat, drawn a mingled breath.
Mine is the darkness of remembered light;
Mine is the conscious and the living death.

Two become one. Yet, tear the one in twain,
How strange there should not two, but halves remain!

OF THE SCHOOL

OURS

School by the bend in the river
Our school
Blue water, tide in
Marsh grass, tide out
Boats frozen in ice
Bundled for winter
And always a salt breeze blowing
Always the gulls
Swooping low over the patio
Flying high
Past field and track

> *Our school*
> *Ours*
> *Orange leaves in fall covering the walks*
> *Red-gold, rustling*
> *Snow banked high in winter*
> *Bending the spruces*
> *Through open windows in spring*
> *The daydreaming smell of lilacs*

> > *Our school*
> > *Bedford*
> > *Red brick, white trim, blue sky*
> > *Under*
> > *Red stripes, blue ground, white stars*
> > *American*
> > *Noisy, rambunctious, free*
> > *Our school*
> > *Ours*

> > *Reprinted from* **Image**

> > *Westport, Connecticut*
> > *1964 - 1976*

MA TEACHES — PA PREACHES

Ma Cleans Her Room

Ma teaches school, and she does it with all her might. This means she doesn't do anything else. She doesn't get meals. Father does. She doesn't clean the house. Ollie does. She doesn't fix zippers or mend pants or sew on buttons. No one does. All Ma does is teach school.

Ma's seniors all graduate this Saturday, and after that, Ma says, she's going to clean her room. This is a major task. Ma's room hasn't been cleaned since school started last September. Ollie comes in once a week and changes the bedding and pushes a dry mop around the middle of the floor. That's all she can do because the walls are banked high with cartons of uncorrected papers and jobs Ma's going to get to someday. So, when Ma says she's going to clean her room, Lorna makes plans to visit friends at the beach for a few days, Pam offers to babysit for Mrs. Race for a week without pay, and I cut my hourly rate for mowing lawns in half.

We do this because Ma likes to clean her room by sitting in the middle of the bed and pointing. "Drop those at the cleaner's, dear, on your way to church," she'll say to Father, pointing to a four-foot pile of winter coats, or "Put that orange and black stuff into the Hallowe'en box, Pam," or "John, carry that pile into the attic. Put 'em in the rummage barrel. Gained so much I can't get into any of 'em, and heaven only knows when I'll lose any."

When Ma tackles the floor of her closet, though, Lorna and Pam both have to be on hand. Forty pairs of shoes must be mated and tried on. All year Ma herself wears only about four pairs of shoes. The other thirty-six are shoes people gave her or shoes she bought at sales six years ago and thought she could squeeze into after they'd been 'broken in a bit,' or shoes Nana sent her from Maine when Aunt Jill died. Now Pam and Lorna must try on all seventy-two odd shoes to see if any fit and can be worn.

"You'll grow into those in a year or so," Ma'll say, pressing down three inches of spare leather above Pam's big toe, or "Those almost fit, Lorna. Just a little loose at the heel."

"When will I ever wear green suede shoes?" Lorna, who's thirteen, wants to know. "With four inch heels?" she adds, wobbling over to look at herself in the mirror. But Ma always has an answer.

"Don't say that. You may be glad to have 'em someday. Why, if I stop teaching school and we have to live on Pa's salary, we'll be lucky if we don't all go barefoot." So Lorna wraps the green shoes in tissue paper and puts them in a carton against the awful day when Ma stops teaching school and we all go barefoot.

Dresses are even worse. "We could take that in at the seams," she'll say, having slipped a striped size 44 over size 12 Pam. "Or cut off the skirt and make a blouse . . . no, better cut off the blouse, I think, and make a skirt. Stand still, dear, while I put in a few pins . . . put it in the make-over box. When I get my room cleaned, I'm really going to sew."

"Not for me you're not," Pam mutters under her breath. "Not that." She stuffs dress, pins and all, into the Christmas carton. "Stick it in there for some overweight wiseman."

Things go on this way for about a week, with carton after carton being dragged home from the liquor store. Ordinarily Pa never goes into a liquor store, but he gets real friendly with the owner when Ma cleans house because she says they have the cleanest cartons. So *Four Roses*, *Seagram's*, and *Johnie Walker Black Label* are all dragged home, filled with things Ma's going to do someday, and packed in the parsonage attic.

Books are the worst, books and papers. Ma gets sample textbooks from every publisher in the country, and she can't bear to throw away even her old ninth- grade grammar.

"Keep your eye out for bookcases," she tells Father every time the church has a rummage sale or an auction. "Goodness knows, this parsonage needs more bookcases!"

"Where'll you put 'em?" he asks, scanning the overflowing shelves filling every wall.

"There's space up there," Ma points to an empty foot or so close to the ceiling. "And sit down a minute, dear, before you go. I want to read you something."

Mother can never bear to throw away a set of themes. She loves all her students and thinks there's at least one Steinbeck and one Hemingway in every class. Pa sits patiently on the edge of the bed.

"Listen to what Charles writes about 'Death' — this might help you with your Easter sermon, dear — tell you what people really want to know: 'Why does the minister pray over the body at a funeral and ask God to take the soul to heaven? The guy's been dead three days. Where's the soul been all this while? Just buzzing around in space waiting for the minister to say a pray —' Don't go, dear. There's lots more. This is what people really want —" But Father, shaking his head, is off down the stairs to make his parish calls. Ma carefully packs away a carton of themes. I mark it Sacred Writ and drag it into the attic.

So Ma cleans her room, and Ollie is happy and waxes the whole floor and washes the curtains, since she can now get at the windows.

But what happens the next week? Next week the cartons of themes and books and clothes too big and clothes too small and Easter costumes and Christmas costumes and stuff to be given away and stuff to be kept all have to be dragged back into Ma's room again. Why? Because Ma has decided to clean the attic — and how can you clean an attic if you can't even climb into it?

Who Remembers Herbie Prescott?

There's only one thing Ma hates to let go of more than books. That's people. She collects them through the years. Parishioners from Pa's old churches, students from her English classes, relatives from Cornwall who visited fifteen years ago just before I was born — Ma has all their names in her big Christmas address book and hangs onto every one. The only time she makes an X before a name is when someone dies.

Ma especially collects old boy friends. She went to the University of Maine — eight boys for every girl, she tells my sisters with a grin — when she was only sixteen, but she didn't marry Pa till she was twenty-seven, so there's about a ten-year span in there when Ma was knee-deep in men.

These old boys are always turning up when we move to a new church or writing long mournful letters to Ma when their wife dies, or showing up with a new wife for her to cast her eagle eye over. When they shake hands with me, they're astonished that Ma has a son taller than they are, and they all like Pa. He greets them tolerantly and tries to cheer them up, and after they leave, he'll say: "Seemed like a real nice feller, dear. Why didn't you marry that one?"

"Oh," Ma'll say, giving Pa that special look, "he's an engineer. Never liked to stop the car and look at sunsets, like you, dear."

"Umm —" Pa'll give her the look right back and maybe a smooch down the neck. "Bet he liked to stop the car *after* sunset, though." Then after dinner Pa'll say something about turning in early tonight, and he and Ma'll wander off upstairs, leaving us three kids to do the dishes.

Not that we don't know how — to do dishes and most everything else around the house. Ma believes in never doing a thing she can teach some kid to do. In Maine where she grew up, people do a lot of fishing, and Ma has a bunch of old sayings about fish. "Eat your fish, John. It's brainfood!" when she cooks mackerel, which I hate. Or "Fish and visitors stink after three days" when Lorna's friends hang around too long. But her favorite is "Give him a fish and he eats for a day. Teach him to fish and he eats for life." Ma is determined that my sisters and I are going to eat for life, so we've been taught, from early on.

We know exactly what to do if we come home from school and find Ma talking to people in the living room. Little typed lists are taped up all over the kitchen in places you'd hardly notice if you weren't looking. The one for *Tea — Unexpected* is taped to the bottom half of the refrigerator door where even Pam, who's eight, can read it.

> 1. *Fill tea kettle with cold water.*
> 2. *Turn stove to high.*
> 3. *If tray needs polish, give swipe with Gorham's while kettle boils.*

Then, after orders about cups and spoons and napkins,

> 7. *If cookie jar empty, spread peanut butter on crackers.*
> 8. *If no peanut butter, cut up apples and cheese. John, wash your Scout knife first.*

So we all know exactly what to do, and eight or ten minutes after we get off the school bus — our record is seven-and-a-half — in we totter with the big silver tray, polished, loaded, and ready to serve.

People are always astonished, especially old ladies from Pa's church. "Why, Mrs. Grenfell, what wonderful children! We didn't hear you say a word!" Ma'll give us a wink and after they leave, if we've done a good job, she'll whip up a double batch of brownies. Usually we do pretty well. But the time Herbie showed up, we flubbed it completely. Maybe that's why he's the old boy friend I remember best.

Herbie was really Professor Herbert L. Prescott. He and Ma had taught English together for three or four years at Bangor High when they were both fresh out of college — Ma with a Phi Bete key from Maine and Herbie with one from Bowdoin. Now he was an assistant professor at Grinnell way out in Iowa and Ma ran the English department at Hall High. Assistant professors, Ma says, don't make much money, but Herbie always had money enough to call Ma long distance and talk a long time whenever he got divorced, which was twice, and whenever he was writing a textbook for high school kids, which was about every other year.

"Good old Herbie," Ma'd say, hanging up after one of the hour-long phone calls. "We still operate on the same beam."

"*Operate* —" Pa, who'd been keeping the spaghetti sauce hot for an hour, would sputter — "That's the right word. He sure operates on you. Picks your brains. What is it this time — another book?"

"Yes, dear — one for 'gifted' kids. He wants full professor, and it's 'publish or perish,' even in Iowa. Mm — your sauce gets better all the time, dear." But Pa is not to be mollified with one compliment.

"You haven't got time to write another book for Herbie. Why can't he write his own?"

"Oh, he's out of touch . . . thinks kids still read *Silas Marner*, the way they did back in Bangor High. Can't believe they read *Catcher* in Grade 7."

"So what did you tell him?"

"Told him — my, this spaghetti is good, dear —told him I'm teaching Kafka and Camus —"

"What," Pa interrupted, "did you tell him about writing his book?"

"Oh, I don't mind giving him a few ideas," Ma quibbled. "He sends checks, and he gives writing credits. Going to list me as editor."

"Editor! What kind? Last time you wrote half the book and he listed you as copy editor! Why don't you write your own book? And don't tell me again how good the spaghetti is!"

"I might —" Ma was getting a little cross by now, "if I didn't have to coach church plays and run the junior choir and keep this great ark of a parsonage clean!"

Keeping the parsonage clean is the least of Ma's worries — except when company's coming. And when Herbie came — the first time Ma'd seen him face to face since her wedding day — he gave her only one day's notice. All hell — as I'm not supposed to say — broke loose. Ma was on the phone trying to persuade Ollie to come for an extra day when Pa came home.

"What's up?" he asked.

"Herbie coaches the College Bowl team for Grinnell," I told him. "They've beaten everybody out west. They're coming east to take on Trinity."

"Grinnell'll never beat Trinity," Pa prophesied happily about his old college. "They'll get clobbered."

"I don't care who gets clobbered," Ma hung up the phone. "I care about the upstairs bathroom. Ollie's promised to come for half a day and do the downstairs, but he might stay all night, and that bathroom's a disgrace. Any paint money in the church budget?"

"Not a cent." Pa took the robe he wore for weddings out of the hall closet. "Have to hurry back, dear. Wedding rehearsal. Of course, there's plenty of paint, though," he called back from the door. "Left over from the last ten projects."

So Ma took a screwdriver and me down cellar to pry the tops off old paint cans. Quarts, pints, half-pints, red, yellow, green — we opened 'em all and dumped the paint into an empty gallon can, trying to get enough. Lorna, who thinks she's good at art, leaned over the stairs.

"You can't do that," she said. "Some's oil and some's latex. You can't mix oil and water."

"Who says we can't?" Ma answered. "We already have. Rinse the soap out of those four brushes, Lorna, and bring them upstairs. We all have to paint. He's coming tomorrow."

"I can't," Lorna said. "Have to learn my Latin, and Pam can't. She has to learn the seven table."

Ma gave her kind of an icy stare. "Do you recall," she said, "who stayed up half the night last month sewing togas for the Latin banquet? And since when could a Grenfell do only one thing at a time? Julius Caesar could do seven. Hurry up!"

So Lorna painted while Ma taught her *'amo, amas, amat, amamus, amatis, amant,'* and not to rhyme *hoc* with *sock*, and Pam sat on the floor and painted mop boards while we took turns drilling her in the seven table. I climbed the step ladder and painted high up, mumbling *heinous, egregious, reprehensible* — my cheerful words for next day's vocab quiz.

When Pa came home at ten, we'd finished, and Ma was shampooing her spattered hair, trying not to spatter soapsuds on the wet paint. Pa stood in the bathroom door and gave a kind of low moan.

"Oh, no — the one room in the house where I could relax!" The color wasn't very relaxing. It had come out kind of a dark, greenish purple with yellow streaks here and there where Ma hadn't taken time to stir the paint enough.

"Look!" Pam pushed past Pa with a picture she'd fished out of Ma's *M* book. It showed Ma the day she'd graduated from Maine, wearing a cap and gown and carrying a long white peace pipe. "Shall I stand it on the toilet bowl, Ma? It's yellow — matches the streaks!" Ma peered through the lather and couldn't help giggling.

"Go to bed, smarty pants. And put that back where you found it. It's irreplaceable."

"Better leave it in sight," Pa said. "Herbie might not recognize you, dear, with purple hair. Scrub real hard over your left ear."

Herbie was there in the living room talking to Ma when I got off the school bus the next day. Lorna and Pam were in the kitchen, going from wall to wall and muttering to each other.

"What's up?"

"Ulcer," Pam whispered. "Herbie's got an ulcer. He can't drink regular tea."

"Ma says to make cambric," Lorna hissed, looking under the calendar, "but I can't find a list! What in hell is cambric?"

"You don't need a list. It's just hot water, milk, and sugar," I told her, going out to untie Rebel. "Make the water good and hot."

She did. Boiling. Herbie was balancing a plate of Ma's brownies on one knee and a cup of boiling cambric on the other when Rebel bounded in. My dog usually behaves pretty well in the house, but the combination of stranger and chocolate was too much for him. When eighty pounds of boxer lunged for the cookies, the teacup skyrocketed, and so did Herbie — screaming, boiling tea running down both pant legs. He left very shortly thereafter — probably to go buy dry pants for the College Bowl.

Pa came in a few minutes later. We told him, and he rushed upstairs to comfort Ma. She was standing in the middle of the purple bathroom, her hands on her hips, looking like a thunder cloud.

"He didn't even," she told Pa coldly, "go to the bathroom."

"Good thing," he said cheerfully. "Might've done worse than wet his pants. Probably vomited. Here, John —" Pa pulled a ten-dollar bill from his pocket. "Take the wedding money and bike over to the hardware, son. Buy two gallons of good white wall paint."

"Two?" Ma protested. She usually got the weddings money for hats and stuff. "Will it take two gallons?"

"To cover this mess," Pa said, "at least — two gallons and two coats."

It did. We painted off and on for days. Trinity beat Grinnell, Pa gloated, and Herbie never showed up at the parsonage again.

He phoned, though, whenever he ran out of ideas for his books, until his ulcer finally caught up with him.

About dusk one day in December I came home from school and found Ma at her desk, addressing cards. Her big Christmas book was open to the *P* page and her eyes were kind of red.

"Don't feel bad, Ma." I put my hand on her shoulder. "Remember what Joe said." I'd kicked up quite a fuss about leaving my friends the last time we'd moved, and Ma'd made me read *Great Expectations*. I liked Joe better than Pip. She looked up and smiled.

"You really remember what Joe said?"

"Sure — 'Life's made up of ever so many partings.' Right?"

"Right." Ma patted my hand. "But he was such an old, good friend. And a brilliant teacher. He had polio, you know, when he was a child. That's why he was so crippled."

So Ma made the *X* by Herbie's name. Like I said, that's the only time she crosses people off, when they die. I can tell she doesn't think it's for good, though. Not even then.

TEACHER

"Read us your poem." He waits expectantly,
Ignores the trembling voice, the nervous hand,
The trochee where the anapest should be,
Mixed metaphor, and meter poorly scanned.

Leaning, he seems to fan the feeble verse,
To cup not only ear, but heart and mind
Around each flickering word, as though to nurse
A blazing flame from fire too long confined.

His eyes intent, his manner kind and mild,
He listens lovingly, as one extends
Both hands toward a toddling child
And calls 'Come walk! You can . . .' The poem ends.

What will the teacher say? A silence, then —
"Well, now, that's fine!" The poet breathes again.

Reprinted from **Renaissance**

JEWISH MOTHER

Carol invites her aged teacher to lunch.
I remember her when, a gawky sixteen, she first
Discovered Freud, decided Hamlet had
An Oedipus complex:
      "Honestly, Mrs. G.,
It's so obvious!" *Then, using the word she'd learned,*
"That incestuous bedroom scene!"
         Poised and beautiful now,
She brings mother, daughter, says:
        "Honestly, Mrs. G.,
I'm such a Jewish mother! You'd never believe!
When Julie was born and I heard my mother scream,
'Carol, you have a daughter!' I thought two thoughts:
'I don't have to worry about her going to war!
All I have to worry about is who she'll marry!'
And Carol grins her deprecatory grin . . .

'She remembers possessive before the gerund,' I thought,
'Forgets her who-whom —'
       "Honestly, Mrs. G.,
The cord wasn't even cut, and already yet
I'm worried about my future son-in-law!
I'm a perfect Jewish mother, don't you think?"

What I think, dear Carol, is that you should not worry.
Teach Julie her **Hamlet,** *her* **Oedipus,** *and with you*
As her beautiful mother, she'll surely make her switch,
Marry good Jewish doctor or lawyer — who cares which?

TEACHING AT HALL

*When we did **Beowulf,** we had a Mead Hall*
 heated cider in the Home Ec room
 stirred in honey
 pretended to be tipsy
And Mike Kaye put up signs all over the room:
 BED AND BOARD — 1 shilling
 BED AND BAWD — 2 shillings
And for one whole week everyone called the teach
Grendel, Dragon Mother . . . .

*And when we read **Two Cities,** the girls brought in*
 steel needles, red wool
 sat knitting long scarves
 hating DeFarge, adoring Carton
Until exam day, when everyone came in shouting,
"It was the worst of times!"
*And for a month before **Native,** we saved all our bones —*
steak bones, chicken bones, fat greasy ham bones —
and on November 5th built a great bone-fire,
 danced around it, tossed on bones,
 *shrieking, yelling, **"A Penny for the Guy!"***
till a neighbor called the fire department and the police . . .

*And when we did **C and P,** no one could remember*
how the vowels went in Dostoievski's name
 till Nan Slonim shouted,
 "O I E V — Oh, I Enjoy Vodka!"
 and after that no one forgot . . . .

And when Camus was killed in his little sports car,
Everyone was quiet because we all knew
 something beautiful and existential
had gone from the world forever
*and some of us read **Fall** over again . . . . .*

*And when **Camelot** came to the Bushnell, we went*
 because of JFK and because
 ***Once and Future** was our favorite book . . .*
*And when Yale did **Macbeth,** we went*

90 of us, through a blizzard . . .
*And when B.U. did **Crucible,** we went,*
     and there was Arthur Miller in the fifth row with the wife
     after Marilyn . . . .

And the day before vacation
when all Stanley's choirs went up and down the corridors
*singing **Deck the Halls** and **Joy to the World***
     Elaine Rosenstein and Mimi Fogelman
     stood in the doorway of 212
     tears streaming down their cheeks because, they said,
"We're seniors. It's our last Christmas!"

And on New Year's Eve there was always Open House
at 612 Fern and last year's seniors
came back from Yale and Brown and Smith
and Holyoke and Harvard and Rensselaer
to show off a bit, and because it's always good
     to have a place
     to come back to . . .
And everyone laughed and talked and ate
the chocolate birthday cake Joan Shapiro always brought
     for Mrs. G.
     who went to bed happy that night because, they told her,
"You taught us all the right things.
Other kids know the titles, but you made us
read the books . . . ."

And W.H.H.H.S.
under Rives and Dunn
and Stearns and Leavitt and Robinson and Dyber
Hoffman and Fraser and Freer and Schwendenwein
Richards and DiFrancesco, Deacon and Moore
and five dozen others equally good
     was a hard-working school
     a proud school
     a great school
because all those people happened to like kids
and teaching at Hall
     was fun . . . .

"OF COURSE, WE WANT HIM TO GO TO HARV—"

The woman cornered me as I dashed down the stairs for lunch. I had twenty minutes to go down two flights, fill my tray, eat, and get back for my 5th period class.

"I wanted to ask you what I can do to help Jon with his English. He's only getting a C, as you know, but everyone tells me you're such a hard teacher your C's are really A's. Now I've been to Plimpton's and bought him a typewriter, erasable bond, a dozen ball points in different colors, paper clips, brads, paste, glue, erasers — hard and soft — posterboard, staples, a stapler, pencils — plain and colored — crayons, a loose leaf notebook, a three-hole punch, a brief case, file cards, rubber bands, desk lamp, construction paper, letter guides — but I'm sure he'll need many other things in your class —"

"Well, really," I stammered, "He seems to be well pre—"

"We bought him an unabridged dictionary — *teflon fabrication, umbilical towers*, all those new space-age words coming out every day —"

"You don't get too many of those in English lit—"

"Of course, he has his old *World Book* from Sedgwick, and my *Americana* in twelve volumes. Should I buy him the *Compton's* with colored pictures? He has a *Roget*, naturally, and a rhyming dictionary, in case you have them write poetry, and we've kept all the old *Geographics* and *Saturday Reviews* and *Harper's*, but we threw out the *Reader's Digest*. Should we have kept the *Reader's Digest*?"

"There isn't too much about English literature in —"

"His father went through his bookshelves, and I went through mine — all the English we had at Brown and Vassar. Chaucer, Milton, Wordsworth — why, some of the books looked like new! Of course, we were dating at the time, and Poughkeepsie is so far from Prov— well, at any rate, we had to buy Jon another bookcase. Put it right beside his desk, so he doesn't have to waste time crossing the room. I mean — all he has to do is *reach out*! His father and I are so excited about doing English lit all over again with Jon! Really reading the stuff, at last! Why, last night we had a poetry party — lay on the rug by the fire and did the witch scenes from *Macbeth* — 'Where hast thou been, sister? Killing swine!' It was really quite scary, and a bit uncomfortable, but Jon said you recommended it. Of course, he wasn't there — had to run over to Plimpton's for Scotch tape to cover his book! Can't think how I forgot Scotch tape — it's so essen—"

I was getting hungrier by the minute, and the minutes were going fast. "I have only a short time —"

"To prepare them for the SAT's? I know! Every minute counts, doesn't it! Jon only got 400 last time, but his father and I both feel that's not *truly* indicative of his *true* ability. We bought *Barron's*, and I hear twenty words every night while his father loads the dishwasher — that way the whole family is involved. And we made Jon give up his afterschool job at Ho-Jo's. I reminded him Hall seniors won thousands of dollars in scholarships last year, and it's certainly better to pick up thousand-dollar scholarships than fifty-cent tips. We're perfectly willing to buy tickets to the plays you recommend, though, I confess, it does mount up. Last week we drove to Yale for *JB*, and Saturday Jon saw *Tartuffe* at Trinity. Friday night we watched Art Carney in *Our Town* on TV — Jon wanted to go to the basketball game, but we really have our priorities straight — and Sunday we saw *Doll's House* —"

"Norwegian," I tried to say, "French, American —" but she did not hear.

". . . really keeps me busy reading the *'What's Going On'* page in the *Courant* . . . so much drama in the Hartford area. But we don't want Jon to miss a thing. I've written overseas for four British magazines — Mrs. DeGroat gave me a list — of course, they haven't started coming yet, but we're keeping a vertical file in one of the kitchen drawers on everything British we run across in Ameri—"

"I really must run —" I said in a loud voice.

"But you haven't told me a thing I can do to help Jon! There must be something! I wrote to British Information in New York, and they sent loads of posters. We put them all up in Jon's room. Of course, his father and I aren't traveling anywhere till we get Jon through Harv— er, college. I've written friends in Devon to send pictures of the Hardy Country, and we didn't miss a single Shakespeare play at Stratford last summer — we knew Jon was going to have you — and we never eat in front of the TV. I mean, we really make mealtime count! We discuss! Why, sometimes Jon can hardly get a word in edgewise, and time just flies! Oh — what a loud bell! Is that the bell for your lunch?"

"No. That's the bell for my 5th period class —"

"But what can I do to help Jon? I really want to, and you haven't told me —"

"LEAVE HIM ALONE! LEAVE HIM ALONE! LEAVE HIM —"

"Stop screaming, darling . . . can't leave you alone." My husband shook my arm. "You said to let you nap only an hour . . . aren't you speaking at Parent-Teachers tonight?"

MOON LANDING

Calling G-O-D . . . Reception clear and strong . . .
Come in, God . . . Pleased? Reports improved, You say?
You've been patient, God . . . The climb has been hard and long
From amoeba slime to the walk on the moon today.

We swung by the tail for a million chattering years?
Scuttled back to the dim, dark caves again and again?
Let retrojets of a million crawling fears
Slow down Your count? . . . God, we are only men!

Not men? . . . Not yet? In blasts of childish pique
We fly by wire? . . . Resist Remote Control? . . .
Pick up Your Homing Beacon very weak? . . .
Question Your Flight Plan? . . . Doubt the Charted Goal?

Still, the word is **GO?** *. . . We read You — strong and clear!*
Steady on course! It looks real good from here!

July 20, 1969

Reprinted from **Renaissance**

COME ALONG, JOSH

A damn health hazard? I understand, sir!
Yes, sir! Right away, sir,
But if I'd known about this job the day we enlisted . . .
Easy on the gas! Easy does it!
The day Tom and I sailed over the bay in my boat,
and Josh came running down to the dock,
put his foot on the stern . . .
Back it up! Back it up! Can't go at it head on!
How many gears on the damn thing anyway —
—put his foot on the stern as we shoved off.
"Room for me?" he grinned.
"I'm going over to sign up, too,
now we're graduated."
I looked at Tom. He was scowling, fumbling with the rope.
I took a deep breath . . .
Take a deep breath! Not if I can help it!
Not here — not now in this unholy stink —
How many years they been lyin' here anyway?
"Sorry, Josh," I said, "No room.
My boat only holds two —" and shoved off,
leavin' him standing there on the dock
alone
the grin gone from his face . . .
Faces! Faces! They got no faces!
Empty eyes and grinnin', grinnin' teeth . . .
Don't grin at me, damn you!
What the hell's so funny? What's the joke?

We picked up the breeze real fast that day,
I felt cold spray on my face,
licked my lips, tasted salt . . .
After awhile I looked back over the wake..
He was still standing on the dock
alone.
Tom saw him, too, and scowled again.
"Damn creep," he said. "Always pushin' in
where he's not wanted
"Yeh," I said. "Always pushin' in . . ."
'Push 'em in, push 'em in!' the Sergeant says.
'Damn health hazard!' the Sergeant says.
'See them big birds up there?' the Sergeant says.
'Well, they ain't chickadees,' the Sergeant says.

Gulls followed us half-way to Portland that day —
the grey gulls of Maine against the grey blue sky . . .
screechin', swoopin', circlin' — hopin' we'd fling
our sandwich crusts on the water . . .
Hundreds of gulls on our island,
hundreds of gulls. . .
but not many Jews. . . not many Jew families
When had Josh come? March?
and followed Tom and me around all spring, hungry
begging the crust of friendship.
They say it's the same other places —
Auschwitz, Buchenwald, Dachou . . .
My friend Josh, where are you now?

I'd have let you come in our boat that day, Josh,
that blue white day
with the white sail scudding over the bay —
I'd have said 'Hop in' and what the hell if Tom scowled
if I'd known about this . . .
I'd sailed three in my boat plenty of times
And you knew it . . . and furthermore,
I'd never have checked
'Mechanically inclined' on that damn form
if I'd known it meant jobs like this . . .

Don't jam, damn you!
What the hell's a bulldozer for if not to bury bones?
Bones, bones, mountains of bones . . .
Nobody in God's world could ever untangle 'em . . .
I was a gravedigger once before
come to think of it . . .
the time we read Hamlet in old Smith's class . . .
"Act it out," she said, "in front of the class. . .
You and Tom be the gravediggers. Josh, you be Hamlet . . .
Get down on your hands and knees, boys.
Girls, stop giggling! It's only make-believe!"

We got down on our knees behind her desk for the grave
and all the girls squealed
when we tossed up the skulls —
made 'em in art class for a joke,
wheat paste and wet newspaper —
and old Smith squealed loudest of all
when a wet one landed right in her lap . . .
Funny how women'll squeal over a little thing like that —
Crumple 'em up! Toss 'em away!
Skulls are made of papier mache!
Make-believe, old Smith? What's that you say?
Take another look and gimme an A!
I'm a helluva gravedigger today!
It was Yorick's skull landed in old Smith's lap —
Yorick, the king's funny boy.
I can still see Josh picking up the damn thing,
holding it, tenderly, as if it were alive . . .
"Yorick," he said . . .
and all the girls stopped squealing
and everything was quiet, listening to the voice
of the Jew,
the liquid voice of the Jew . . .
Is that why you hated him, Tom?
'cause he was always Hamlet,
'n you 'n I were only a couple o' gravediggers?
Clowns — they called us in the book. Was that why?

"Alas, poor Yorick," Josh said, in the liquid voice,
"I knew him well . . .
Why, he hath carried me on his back a thousand times . . ."
I knew you, too, Josh, but not very well,
And I wish you'd get the hell off my back!
What are you doing on my back anyway?
It was Hitler killed you, not me!
You and six million like you — Jews!
Every damn Jew he could get his damn hands on . . .
What is a Jew, anyway?
We studied about Jews once in Sunday School . . .
David was a Jew —
the guy with the slingshot who wrote poetry:
'The Lord is my shepherd, I shall not want . . .
He maketh me to lie down in green pastures . . .
He maketh me to lie down in gas chambers . . .
He maketh me to lie down in deep trenches . . .
Surely my trench overfloweth. . .'
That's the last damn pile, soldier.
So pour on the drum o' gasoline, soldier.
But don't toss the match quite yet, soldier,
Till I get the hell outta the way, soldier.
What is a Jew, anyway?
Moses was a Jew, a little Jew kid,
hidin' out on the river so he wouldn't get killed . . .
Auschwitz, Buchenwald, Dachou —
We killed 'em then! We kill 'em now!
Saw a burnin' bush once, Moses did.
Got all excited. Said God
Was inside the bush, inside the burnin' fire . . .
Stick around, Moses! Don't go away!
You'll see more'n a measly bush burnin' in a minute!
You'll see one helluva blaze in a minute!
Stick around! . . . Wow! What a blaze!
Bones, bones burnin' bright
Like a tiger in the night . . .
Who's inside this one, Moses? God? No — not God.
The Devil himself's in this one, Moses —
Adolph 'n Eichmann 'n me 'n the whole rotten world's
in this one! . . . but not God. Not God at all.

I was a Jew once
in the Christmas pageant, the year I was ten.
Had to climb a ladder backstage,
Stick my head out the window way up high.
The Innkeeper — that was me.
Had to holler down to Joseph 'n Mary when they came along —
"No room! No room for you in this inn!" I said.
"Go somewhere else to be born," I said.
"No room for you in my boat!" I said.
"My boat only holds two —"
And the Christmas angels sang for joy . . .
Herod will kill each little Jew boy . . .
I heard the bells on Christmas Day. . .
Their old familiar carols play . . .
Fly to Egypt! Do not stay!
Christ! What a blaze!
Jesus was a little Jew baby.
Jesus was born a little Jew baby.
"I'll come again," he said.
"I'll come again. Can't say exactly when."
Were you born again, little Jew baby?
In a different town? Dachou, maybe?
Who the hell's buried in this damn trench?
Who the hell's burnin' here anyway?

CHRIST

Come along, Josh . . . get in my boat.
I've carried three in my boat
plenty of times . . .
Come along, Josh . . . please?

Suffield Writers Conference, 1959
Best Stream-of-Consciousness Poem

Reprinted from Renaissance

HIS LIFE HAS JUST BEGUN

"You know," Philip Tirabassi said to me the last day of school, two days before his death, "I'm going to be a teacher for the next forty years. I never want to be anything else." Phil was a teacher for only the next forty-odd hours, but he was fully, devotedly, enthusiastically a teacher for all the hours allowed him. I remember him as a teacher in many different ways.

I can see Phil — nervous, tense, trying too hard to pound in the vocabulary lesson — standing before the class as I, his department head, made my first 'evaluative' visit to his classroom. I can see him running up the stairs at the close of school an hour later.

"How did I do? What did I do wrong? Why was I so nervous?" Phil wanted to be the best English teacher in the world, and he was willing to learn how. He was teachable. One had only to suggest a method, a technique, for Phil to seize it, shape it with his individual touch, adapt it to the needs of his individual students. During his first year at Hall, I would often look up from my desk to see him in the doorway, lesson plans under his arm. "Would you go over these with me, Mrs. G.? I want to make sure I'm on the right track." He was constantly coming with a new book, a new recording, the announcement of a play.

I can see Phil standing knee-deep in a snowbank on a blustery January day in New Haven, counting off Hall students as they boarded the bus for home. New Haven was officially in a State of Emergency, but we had brought two bus loads through the blizzard to see the Yale School of Drama production of *Macbeth*.

I can see him at University of Connecticut doing the same thing, the night we took eighty students to Storrs for *Romeo and Juliet*. I recall the consternation in his voice when I telephoned him at one-thirty the next morning.

"Was Jan McNulty on your bus, Phil? Her mother just woke me. Jan hasn't come home." Yes, he was sure he'd checked off Jan — but wouldn't it be the child of the President of the Board of Education who got misplaced! Where could she be? We'd been home two hours! How relieved we both were when Mrs. McNulty phoned back a few minutes later. Jan had just strolled in, her mother said. She'd been having pizza with the gang at the diner. Yes, she'd had a wonderful evening!

Hall students always did, with Mr. T. Under his tutelage many who had never before seen a live play clamored to be in the musicals he directed at Hall, developed a lifelong interest in the theater.

All such group excursions, of course, took place outside of school hours. All were extra-curricular, extra labors of a devoted teacher.

I can see Phil in the doorway of my home, bags of groceries in his arms, one night when I had missed a few days of school because of a cold. He had come with what he called 'a gift from the English Department' — frozen TV dinners, steaks, fruit, and a bunch of flowers atop one bag.

"Nothing hard to cook," he grinned at my husband, who knew that if he said the word, Phil would take off his jacket and cook the dinner himself. Whatever the occasion — flowers and food for the sick, gifts for bride or groom, anniversary remembrances — Phil's hand was usually the first to reach for his billfold. He believed wholeheartedly in the personal touch, the intimate concern that transform a professional school staff into a warm school family.

One of Phil's great pleasures during the last months of his life came in instigating and planning a testimonial dinner in honor of our retiring principal, Henry J. Rives. Mr. Rives was admired and loved by all his staff, but Phil's feeling, sincere and honest, bordered on veneration. Indeed, this young man, who came to Hall from Colby College when he was barely twenty-one, treated all older teachers with unbounded love. He could not do enough to honor us, could not take steps enough to help us, simply because we were teachers. To some weary ones, his dedication and enthusiasm restored dreams and visions of our calling that we had lost along the way. Philip Tirabassi made us feel again, because he himself felt it so keenly, the excitement and challenge of working with the volatile stuff that is the youth of America. So, as from our experience we tried to help him, he from his youth helped us by restoring our faith in the value of our common task — guiding, leading, teaching the young.

Phil loved to buy things. I have a memory of him strolling up and down the aisles of the supermarket across from Hall. I saw him — the night before his tragic death by drowning — picking out delicacies for the picnic that was to celebrate his first wedding anniversary.

"Hi, Mrs. G.," he called, dropping a can of fancy anchovy paste into his wire basket. "You know —" he stopped a moment to chat — "I've had more fun this year buying things to eat! Di thinks I'm crazy, and, of course, half the stuff sits in the refrigerator and never gets finished, but I love to try new things!" He chose another jar of 'genuine-imitation' caviar and walked on, grinning.

Last winter, overwhelmed with mid-year examinations, I mentioned to Phil that my son John had written from college that he desperately needed new shirts — a hidden black sock in the dormitory automatic had ruined all his. "What's his size?" Phil asked, "and his favorite color?" Phil had mid-year exams to correct, too, but he went to the store and picked out the shirts, went to the post-office and mailed the package. John wrote to say the shirts were great, that my taste was getting quite ivy-leaguish. Phil, himself always impeccably dressed, had, of course, chosen exactly the right thing.

One day, I recall, he asked me the best place to shop for a sofa bed, said he had company coming. "Buy a cheap one," I advised cynically. "Then the company won't stay too long."

He looked at me without smiling. "I want the best one I can find," he said. "It's for my father and mother." Phil loved his Maine family and, because he knew my home, too, is in Maine, often talked of his parents, his married sister, his younger brother. We agreed the air changes instantly for the better once one crosses the bridge between Portsmouth, New Hampshire, and Kittery, Maine. Phil was grateful to all Maine people who had helped him get his education and eagerly wrote letters of recommendation for Hall students wanting to go to Colby, Bates, Bowdoin, or Maine. It is fitting that the Philip W. Tirabassi Scholarship has been established by his students, friends, and fellow teachers.

Finally, I have two vivid pictures of Phil in relation to his church. With many other Hall teachers, I attended his and Diane Powers' beautiful wedding ceremony at the Church of Saint Mark the Evangelist. I can see his slight figure kneeling at the altar as he made his promises to Diane and his vows to God. A year and three days later we went to the same church and saw more than two hundred grieving Hall students form an Honor Guard for the slow movement of a flower-decked casket.

Phil is buried in Fairview Cemetery, a few hundred yards from my home on Fern Street. Now that the leaves are gone, I can see from my windows the slope where he lies. Several times since June I have gone there Sunday afternoons with flowers from church or garden. Almost always I have found Hall students, walking around, searching for his grave, for as yet there is no marker. I help them find the spot, and they sit down on the grass, talk quietly or keep silent.

Yes, here in the town where he lived and laughed and loved and worked the brief two years of his life as a teacher, Philip Tirabassi is remembered in many different ways by many different people. If I had to chose one word to epitomize his personality and character, it would be the word *kind*. Giving himself without stint, pouring out his exuberant strength and great talent to help people, Phil was innately kind.

And he was humble. Despite his many rare abilities, he drove himself always to be better. Knowing that his junior students would probably be my senior students this year, he came a month before school closed, asking to borrow my planbook overnight.

"I want to check through," he said, "to see whether I've missed anything."

"But, Phil," I remonstrated, "you don't have to teach them everything! Leave something for me to do!"

"I know," he laughed, "but I want to make sure they're well prepared."

I have Phil's former students now, and they are well prepared. They are better prepared than is the fortune of many to be, because for a year they sat in the classroom of a truly dedicated teacher. Their student essays reveal with the honesty and clarity of the young the lessons learned from that teacher — lessons far beyond the scope of syntax, rhetoric, and literary analysis. I am certain that his influence will live on in hundreds of classrooms, for more than one of his students tell me that because of him, they, too, plan to become teachers.

And so, Philip Tirabassi will, in truth, be a teacher 'for the next forty years,' as he wanted to be. His life as a teacher has not ended. It has just begun.

September, 1962

DIALOGUE

Year after year they come and fill the rows
Of seats before me — faces, rounded, square,
Dull, eager, stupid, bovine, or aglow.
We look — I at them and they with one accord
At me, and all is tense, taut questioning.
For we must live together, they and I,
Liking it or no, long days.

                "She looks tough," *some say,*
And others, **"Gee, I hope she c'n take a joke!"**
And some, **"I don't give a damn. They all hate me,**
'Cause I'm dumb, 'n I'll flunk anyway."

                        I hear their words,
And do they, too, hear mine?

                "This is the age
Of the machine, but these are not machines.
These faces, bright or stupid, all have life —
Life with its infinite power for good and bad,
Young life, and plastic, that I shall help mold . . .
Less than movies, perhaps, TV, radio, pop stars;
Yet my touch will tell, for these lives are not old
But sensitive still to every passing hand . . ."

Their clear eyes search me yet, and in their gaze
Thoughts inarticulate but deeply felt:
"You who are lazy must exact hard work.
You who procrastinate must teach us speed.
You who are cowardly must courage give . . ."
Their thoughts a challenge, I must answer make —
My only answer a confessional:
"I in whom ardor's dead must draw forth zeal,
I who am crude, give you a culture fine.
I who tell lies with fluent, social ease
Must make you glad to give your lives for truth."

A gong sounds. **"Come to order, class,"** *I say.*
How dare I be a teacher, anyway?

Reprinted from the **Bangor Daily News**

OF THE CHURCH

COMMUNION AT THORNTON HEIGHTS

For the Reverend Dr. John Millard Grenfell

This is the place where I am most at home,
Am most at peace, most nearly my own self,
The place — though I may not know a name, a face —
Where I lean back on my own family,
Lean back on God . . . look up through vaulted space
Above the altar there, the wine, the bread,
And feel myself uplifted, nurtured, fed
On grace. This is the place, the place.

I hear

Around me all the rise and fall of sound,
Cadence of murmured prayer, petition, praise,
The pulse of organ, anthem, soaring hymn:
"Lift up your hearts! We lift them up . . ."

Silent,

Myself too maimed for words, I listen for
The timeless words that minister to me:
"Ye that do truly, earnestly repent . . .
Give us this day . . . my body, broken for thee . . ."
No sham, pretense . . . all, all are sinners here —
"Not worthy so much as to gather up the crumbs" —
Humble before a God who knows, yet loves,
Who judges, yet absolves, and most of all
Gives courage to go on — ". . .that ye may walk
In newness of life, may grow, may dwell in him."

In all the world

This is the place where I am most at peace,
Am most myself, the self I want to be.
This place in all the world is home to me.

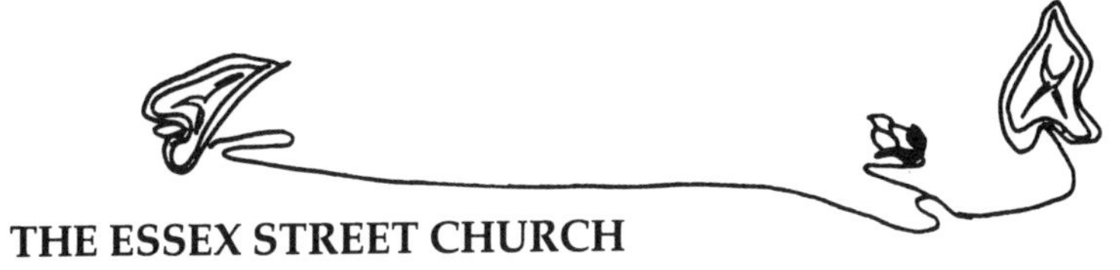

THE ESSEX STREET CHURCH

Political analysts have spent years on the 1976 presidential election, trying to figure out why we Americans voted as we did. They didn't need to spend a minute analyzing my vote. I would have told them. It was because of the Essex Street Baptist Church in Bangor, Maine.

No, it's not my home church. In fact, I haven't been in it for more than fifty years and was there then only four times for a total of perhaps four hours. I remember those hours, though. They were vibrant, noisy, warm, soul-stretching, and powerful — powerful enough to reach across half a century and make my bred-in-the-bone, Maine Republican arm pull that Democratic lever for the first time.

No, we six Coffin kids growing up on Outer Broadway were not Baptists, but baptized Methodists. Certificates framed in black and bearing impressive signatures hung on our bedroom walls. But the year I was ten and my sister Jill eight, we were the only Coffins attending Sunday School. Our younger brothers, Millard and Bart, were too small for the two-mile walk. Our older brothers, Merle and Lloyd, thought they were too big. They liked Sunday night Epworth League with its girls and games — Wink 'em, Post Office, and Spin-the-Bottle. But to Jill and me, going to Sunday School was the high point of the week.

We spent most of Saturday getting ready for it — put shiny shoe-blacking on our wide-brimmed straw hats, perked up the pink and blue forget-me-nots around the crown, burned our fingers steaming the wide velvet ribbon that hung down the back. We rubbed Vaseline into our patent leathers and wiped it off again. Our white linen dresses had scalloped sleeves and scalloped skirts, each scallop edged with tatting. Papa had gone forty miles to the Guilford Woolen Mills way up on the Piscataquis to buy the pale peach cloth for our spring coats. Mama had pushed the treadle on her Golden Oak Singer Sewing Machine far into the night to fashion the wide cape collars and tiny pockets into which we stuffed our pennies for the offering.

We liked the way we looked — Jill's gold curls brushed and shining, my stubborn brown ones tamed — as we left home each Sunday and picked our way down the narrow dirt road that was Broadway in 1921. We liked even more the friends we met along the way. Most of all, we liked Dottie Tinker.

Dottie was not a Methodist, but a Baptist. Her mother and our papa sometimes chatted as they rode to business on the Center Street car line. I don't suppose Dottie had ever heard the word *proselytize*, and I'm sure Jill and I hadn't. Nevertheless, each Sunday when we got to our church on the corner of Pine and Somerset, Dottie urged us to keep on going around the corner to hers. Each Sunday we said no, and probably we'd have kept right on saying no if our Sunday School teacher that year had ever been able to say my name. She couldn't. She alternated between *Carline, Charline, and Corinne*. The class waited each week, giggles at the ready, to see what I'd be called that Sunday.

Jill and I even took the trouble to explain to her how I'd got my name.

"Papa wanted to name her Clara, for Mama," Jill said, "but Mama wouldn't let him, 'cause she hates her name —"

"So they just called me 'Baby' for seven months," I said.

"Then one night," Jill interrupted, "Papa went into Crosby's Store, and Mr. Crosby showed him something new. It was fake butter, called oleo-margerine —"

"So Papa hurried home and added *-ine* to *Clara* and called me *Clarine*." I pronounced the names carefully and slowly.

"Margerine!" The teacher laughed. "Fake butter! Do you suppose, dear," she smiled at me, "that's why you're a little on the plump side?" She still smiled, every time she looked at me, and she still called me *Charline* or *Corinne* or *Carline*.

She came hurrying up one Sunday as we stood with some other kids on the corner, Dottie, as usual, urging Jill and me to come along to her church.

"Good morning, boys and girls. Don't be late!" She looked at me and smiled. "Come along, Claxine!"

The *Claxine* did it. The girls tittered. The boys doubled up with laughter. "*Claxine!*" they gasped between giggles. "Come along, *Claxine!*" I grabbed Jill's hand and Dottie's arm and, dragging them both after me, fairly ran around the corner to be a Baptist.

Come, thou Almighty King!
Help us thy name to sing!
Help us to praise! . . .

We could hear the singing way out on Essex Street. Inside a big man with big glasses, a big face, big shoulders, and a big booming voice was standing on a platform waving his arms.

"That's the superintendent, Goucher James," Dottie whispered. "He loves to sing." Dottie marched up on the platform and proudly printed our names on a blackboard under the word *Visitors*. Then she led us over to a corner where a tall, skinny lady with salt-and-pepper hair was singing loudly, too. "Come on! That's our teacher, Mrs. Armstrong." Mrs. Armstrong smiled and passed us her hymnal, open to the right page.

Come and reign over us,
Ancient of Days!

"Now who," Goucher James shouted, "can tell me what 'Ancient of Days' means?" Dead silence. Then a young man, 17 or 18, spoke up.

"Does it mean God's been around for a long time?"

"Right, Clyde! And since you got it right, come up here and sing it for us. A hand for Clyde Jones, everybody!"

Clyde Jones stepped up on the platform. He wore a blue jacket, white linen knickers, and golf hose with a little tassel at each knee. I thought he was beautiful. He opened his mouth and sang, and mine dropped open in astonishment. I had expected a deep voice like my Papa's, but this voice — so high, so clear, so piercing sweet! In those pre-phonograph, pre-radio, pre-movie days, I had never before heard a tenor. I listened breathlessly.

Come, thou Almighty King!
Help us thy name to sing . . .

"Thank you, Clyde! And now let's look at the next verse. Who can explain 'Incarnate Word'?" No one could, so we were told to find out before next Sunday. The service went on. Jill and I were introduced as "Visitors" and urged to come again. Dottie was awarded her two gold stars for bringing us. My sister and I looked at each other guiltily as we dropped Methodist pennies on the Baptist offering plate. Then, as Mrs. Armstrong began the lesson, a handsome blond man came over to our class, his hand outstretched.

"These must be the little Coffin girls. I'm the minister, Mr. Brown. Now which is Lillian?" I nudged Jill and she stuck out her hand. Mr. Brown glanced up at the blackboard. "Then this must be Clarine." I had expected him to stumble over my name, but he didn't. He said it quite clearly. "Now that's an unusual name."

"It was made up," Dottie volunteered with a giggle, "from margerine. That's fake butter." Mr. Brown looked at Dottie and then at me. He still held my hand. I waited to see if he would say anything about plumpness.

"Oh, no, Dottie." He shook his head. "You're mistaken there. Clarine's name has nothing to do with margerine. It comes from the Latin and means light. Clear, shining light. Bright. Even brilliant. You'll study Latin someday, Dottie, when you're older. And aren't you fortunate, Clarine, to have such a beautiful name!" He went off upstairs to the sanctuary, taking my ten-year-old heart with him.

Of course we went back the next Sunday — to hear Clyde Jones sing tenor, Mr. Brown say my name, and to find out about "Incarnate Word." Nobody I'd asked all week seemed to know. Even our teacher at Hillside School said she wasn't much on religion.

Whoever would have guessed it means the Baby Jesus? "'The Word became flesh and dwelt among us,'" Goucher James explained delightedly, as if he were solving a puzzle. *"Incarnate* is Latin for *in the body!"* Latin again! Maybe I'd study Latin, too, along with Dottie. Clyde Jones sang the second verse as a duet with a pretty girl named Katie Boulter. They kept smiling at each other, and Dottie whispered, "That's his girl! I bet they get married!" Mr. Brown stopped by and remembered our names. Mrs. Armstrong invited the class to a party at her house Saturday afternoon.

When Jill and I got home, we asked our Mama if we could go to a Sunday School party at our teacher's home on Saturday. We didn't mention which Sunday School, which class, or which teacher. She said we could, and we did. At Mrs. Armstrong's house I was astonished to see whole walls lined with books. I was looking at *Five Little Peppers* when Dottie came along.

"You aren't supposed to look at other people's books," she said primly. Mrs. Armstrong was right behind her.

"I don't mind if Clarine looks at my books. Would you like to borrow that one, dear?" I raced home after the party, read a third of it before supper, a third after, and the last third under the blankets by flashlight. The next morning, filled with pure gratitude, we walked straight past the Methodist church for the third Sunday.

Jill had joked that "Holy Comforter" in verse three must mean a quilt full of holes, but of course it doesn't. It means, Goucher James told us, the Holy Spirit, always there to comfort us and help us out. The last verse, he said, has a kind of surprise in it.

"Put them all together, and what do we have? God, Jesus, and the Holy Spirit? Why, the great One-in-Three, the Trinity!" He seemed excited, and we sang about the Trinity with triple gusto to please him. And though I've sung "Come, Thou Almighty King" many times in many places since, I've never once sung it without remembering the big, booming voice of Goucher James. It was the first "grown-up" hymn I ever understood.

I gave Mrs. Armstrong back her book. "Finished already? I'll bring you another next Sunday. We'll be taking you off the 'Visitors' list then, you know!" she smiled.

"Taking us off? Why?"

"Because you've been here three Sundays. You're members now. Mr. Brown will be out to call on your parents soon."

Slowly, slowly up Broadway that day. Slowly, slowly through the park, past Crosby's Store. Even slowly past Mae Plummer's house where all her dogs came out to bark at us. How explain to trusting Methodist parents that their two daughters, with Methodist certificates on their bedroom walls, had both turned Baptist?

We didn't have to. Papa happened to chat with Dottie Tinker's mother on the Center Street carline the next day. The Baptists were so pleased, she told him, that the Coffins were coming to their church. Were we all going to be baptized?

We never were. Two of us were chastised, though — our bare legs tickled with little switches Papa made us break off the lilac bush ourselves. My legs harder and longer than Jill's, because I was older. Not, Papa was careful to explain, for going to the Baptist Sunday School, but for deceiving Mama. You could tell a whopping big lie, Papa said, just by keeping your mouth shut.

Whether Papa kept his mouth shut to Mama, we never asked and never knew. I went to the Essex Street Baptist Church only one more time, the fourth time, months later. Mr. Brown, Dottie told us tearfully as we stood on the corner, was leaving the State of Maine, probably forever. Couldn't we come to his farewell service Sunday night? I asked my mother and she said yes, if one of the older boys would go with me, though she couldn't imagine why I wanted to. I promised Lloyd I'd write his next two English themes. He held out for three, and we went.

We got there early. I wanted to sit in the front pew, as close to Mr. Brown as I could get, but Lloyd said no. He was afraid I'd cry and "make a fool of him." He made me climb to the balcony and sit in the back row. I lasted very well through the glowing testimonials, the presentation of the gift, the farewell sermon. I sniffled only once or twice during Clyde Jones's beautiful solo. But the closing hymn was too much for me.

God be with you till we meet again.
By His counsels guide, uphold you,
In His arms securely fold you . . .

My chest heaved. Hot tears scalded my cheeks. "Cut it out!" Lloyd hissed in my ear. "Cut it out or we'll go!" I tried, but I could not.

Till we meet, till we meet,
Till we meet at Jesus' feet . . .

Would I really never see Mr. Brown again on this earth? Sobs racked me. I bawled aloud. Lloyd grabbed me by the arm, yanked me down the narrow balcony stairs, down the wide sanctuary stairs, out into the cold night air of Essex Street, where he dropped my arm and ran for home. I trailed sadly after, the stirring Baptist voices still ringing in my ears — "God be with you till we meet again."

We never did. I stayed a Methodist — became a Methodist minister, married a Methodist minister, mothered a Methodist minister.

But that November I voted for a Baptist. Maybe it doesn't make sense, but I did it as a thank-you to Mr. Brown, who told me my name means clear, shining light; to Mrs. Armstrong, who lent me her book; to Clyde Jones, who sang like an angel; to Goucher James, who taught me the meaning of words — as a thank-you to all those long-ago Baptists who welcomed and enfolded in Christian love two little country kids who came to the Essex Street Church with dusty shoes and pennies in their pockets.

Reprinted from **Christian Herald**

JESUS ONCE A BABY WAS

A Hymn for Junior Choir

Jesus once a baby was,
Once a laughing boy;
Then a man, grown strong and tall,
Spreading peace and joy.
Lord, as we grow, help us all to be
In our work and in our play
Ever more like Thee.

Peace would reign throughout the earth,
Gone be strife and care,
Love would rule in every heart,
Joy be everywhere,
If, as we grew, all would strive to be
In our thoughts and in our deeds
More, O Christ, like Thee.

Once we all were babies small,
Now we're children free.
Soon we will be strong and tall,
Facing life bravely.
Hear, Lord, our prayer, offered reverently,
Make us, as we older grow,
Ever more like Thee.

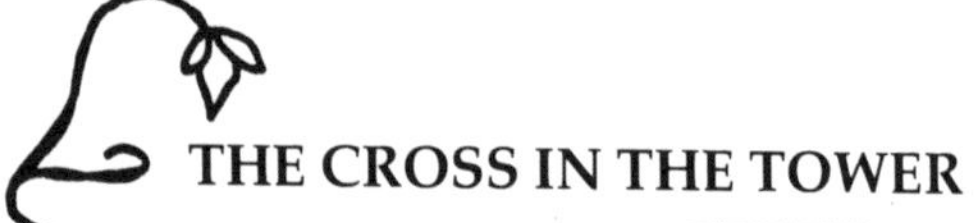# THE CROSS IN THE TOWER

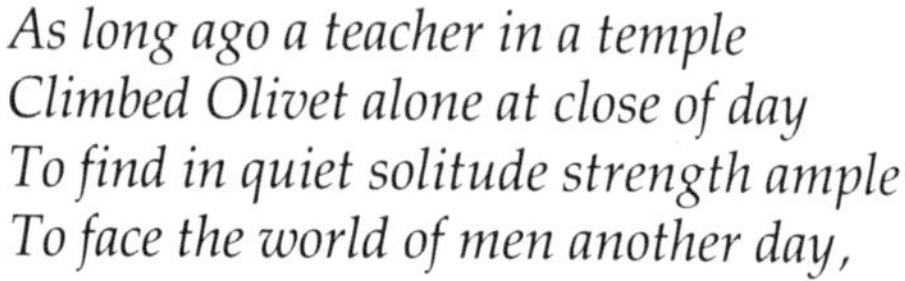

As long ago a teacher in a temple
Climbed Olivet alone at close of day
To find in quiet solitude strength ample
To face the world of men another day,

So do we turn from press of crowded city,
From grasping hands, rapacious, trained to kill,
From cries of pain, from power that knows no pity,
To seek a shining cross upon a hill.

Not that we hate the world of men we're leaving —
More than they love themselves, we love them now.
So we must find the answer to their grieving,
Search for the power to lift the heads that bow.

And as by day we read eternal answers,
By night a cross shines down, lest we forget —
Proud in our books and arrogant with learning —
The answer was a Cross at Olivet.

Hartford Theological Seminary, 1935

PARABLES

Unwilling guests who send polite regrets;
Simon, unmindful of his canceled debts;
Rich fool, who builds a barn, a soul forgets —
These are the parables the Teacher told.

A suffering neighbor carried to a bed;
Repentant tears on weary feet fast shed;
A publican's sore heart and low-bowed head —
These are the ways the laws of God unfold.

Beloved son thrown dead outside the wall;
In dark of night a friend's importunate call;
A fig tree saved to bear another fall —
These are the pictures, vivid, true, and bold

A tired servant cooks his master's meal;
A thief draws near, unguarded goods to steal;
A beggar's sores, dog-lapped, begin to heal —
The scroll of God before men's eyes unrolled.

A coin gleaming in the quick-swept dust;
A steward, most consistent, though unjust;
Tense, anxious words: "Find my lost sheep
          I must!" —
These are the tales that won men's hearts of old.

A proud guest takes the highest seat of all;
A brother sulks outside the festal hall;
A father seeks, forgives, and loves us all —
The simple stories gleam like bits of gold.

The wisest man who ever lived used not
The language of the schools, so soon forgot,
But rather chose his teaching to impart
In the unchanging language of the heart.

STEEP WAS THE ROAD

Steep was the road up Calvary.
He stumbled on. He could not see.
Milady is wearing blue this year
And flowered hats, cocked low on the ear . . .

The young bones scrunched when the nails went through,
And red blood dripped a noonday dew.
"Wire the factory hell! The dirty rats
Promised today a thousand new hats! . . .

His aching throat was parched and dry.
It took so long, so long to die.
"I must have a corsage, dear. All the girls do —
White orchids this year, since my suit is blue . . ."

"This do in remembrance of me," He had said,
Drinking the wine and breaking the bread.
"Why did you bake it, Jane?" he cried.
"You know damn well I like ham fried!"

"He who would my disciple be
Let him take up his cross and follow me."
"Go to church? Hell, no! We stayed abed.
Party last night gave us both a big head!"

Centuries pass. The cross on the hill
Carries its dying burden still.
Blind to its meaning, men nor see nor hear . . .
And milady wears blue, cocked low on the ear . . . . .

*Reprinted from the **Hartford Courant***

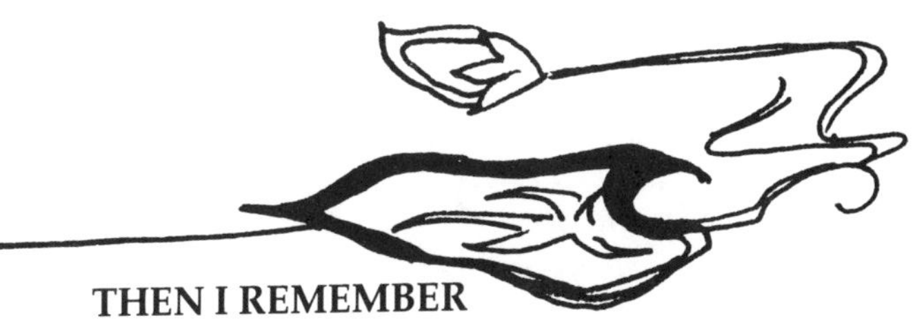

THEN I REMEMBER

Sometime it seems so far away,
That first triumphant Easter Day,
I feel it scarcely real somehow,
So more real is the here and now.

Then I remember with a chill
That Golgotha is any hill,
Jerusalem is any town —
Maybe He's here now, looking down.

Then I remember with a start
Judas may live in any heart
That harbors jealousy or greed,
That's hypocrite in word or deed.

So to my knees I go in prayer
At an altar rail or anywhere
And say, "Christ Jesus, forgive me, too!
I'm one of those who crucified you!

I'm one of those who came and sat,
Spent the three long hours in idle chat!
I'm one of those who just passed by
And said, 'Well, well, we all must die.'

I'm one of those who mocked and railed
And wondered why God's power had failed.
O Master of Life, forgive me, too,
And send me forth God's will to do!"

Reprinted from the **Enquirer**

CARILLON

For Lieutenant Harvey A. Durant
Corporal William D. Shaw, Jr.
Carman Duncan Walker, MM 2/c USNR

When these bells ring out in praise of Thee,
God of Earth and Sky and Sea,
We shall remember — we gave three . . .

Three who died on earth, sky, sea
Willingly that we might be
Free, O God, to worship Thee.

One fell flaming from the skies.
One beneath the cold sea lies.
One from the earth will never rise.

We shall remember and not forget
Three whom we loved . . . we see them yet . . .
Three whom we owe an unpaid debt —

A debt unpaid till war is done,
A debt unpaid till peace is won,
Owed by the living, every one.

Ring, bells, o'er Bethel hills so fair!
Let holy music fill the air!
Call Bethel folk to bow in prayer!

Sound ancient hymn and carol dear!
Lift up the hearts of all who hear!
Give us new courage . . . . cast out fear!

Ring, bells, o'er people, land yet free!
Bless, God, the sound in memory
Of three of ours who are with Thee.

Dedication Service
Veterans' Memorial Chime
Bethel, Connecticut
February 11, 1951

THINGS SEEM DIFFERENT AT EASTERTIDE

Things seem different at Eastertide
When someone dear to you has died.
You think very little about what you'll wear,
But you listen to the preacher when he speaks in prayer.
Yes, things seem different at Eastertide
When someone close to you had died —

You look at the lilies, pure white from blackest earth,
And you think about death and you think about birth,
*And you say, **Christ Jesus, is it really true?***
Does he live? Is he living, somewhere with you?
Those 'heavenly mansions' you went to prepare —
Are they real? Shall I know him someday there?

Yes, things seem different at Eastertide
When someone dear to you has died.

TWO MINISTERS HAVE I

For H. Bartlett Coffin

Two ministers have I. One wears a robe,
Voluminous and black, wide velvet bands
Up, down, around . . . a purple stole embossed
With crosses, crowns, Greek letters in bright gold.
To those who come a-hungering he serves
The wafer and the wine with quick, deft skill,
Or thunders forth the Word full ominously
From massive pulpit high above the heads
Unnamed, unknown in silent pews below.

This minister is an important man —
Flies to important meetings far and near,
Synods, symposia on world affairs,
Attends important councils everywhere . . .
Buries important people, marries, too,
With ritualistic pomp — but if you, even you,
Should have a problem, you can telephone
His office and his secretary'll look
In her important book and set a time
For an appointment at some future date . . .
If you can wait . . . .

Two ministers have I. The other wears
A faded orange shirt, sits chin in hand
At a kitchen table near an unlocked door
And seldom speaks. He listens, though, listens
To all who come and go, and go and come
Day after day, week after week — the maimed,
The well, the young, the old, the rich, the poor,
Hurting or happy — all who come to sit
At a common table, sharing common things:

The joy when a child is born, the sorrow when
One stumbles and falls . . . pride when some honor's won
Some hard-earned goal attained . . . the deep despair
When the job is lost, the diagnosis not
Benign, the loved one dies, the marriage breaks . . .

He listens, hears the halting words, hears, too,
Unspoken words too difficult to say,
Shares silences, offers the bread, the wine,
The outstretched hand, sometimes the folded bill,
And when tears flow, wipes his own tears away.

So if my heart were breaking, I might go kneel
At an altar rail, take the proffered sacrament
From practiced hands, professional and cool . . .
Or I might walk through an unlocked door to sit
By my minister in the faded orange shirt
Who holds my hand in a warm, unyielding grasp
And lets me know he's been there and he cares.

WOMEN OF GOD

To a woman first God did impart
The bursting secret of His heart,
And a woman cried, "I am most blessed!"
As God's Son stirred beneath her breast.
Women followed all the way Christ trod,
Climbed the hills to learn of God,
Brought their babies to be blessed,
Haltingly their sin confessed,
Sacrificed their ointments rare,
Dried His feet upon their hair,
Till, in the shadow of the Cross,
Women wept and knew their loss.

Who came early at break of day?
Who found the death stone rolled away?
Who heard when shining angels said,
"Why seek ye the living among the dead?
Your Lord is risen! Do not fear!
Your Lord is risen! He is not here!"
Who ran to tell with trembling voice
God's great, glad news: "He lives! Rejoice!"

Only a vision? An idle tale?
Two thousand years do not prevail
Against that truth!

                And are God's lips sealed?
Has He no word to be revealed?
No waiting message to impart
This day unto the quiet heart?
False gods cry loud. Beneath their din
The still, small voice yet speaks within.
Who, listening, hears? Who will proclaim
That voiceless truth in Mary's name?
Denying self, forsaking all,
Who follows now the Master's call?

O women of God who in silence pray,
Rise and herald the truth this day!
To women of old and your God, be true!
Let Christ live in the world through you!

Reprinted from the **Signal**
For Freda Eppler, Secretary
Commission on Status of Women
New York East Conference, 1941 - 49

THE FOUR MARYS

A Dramatic Service of Worship

Staging: Use Biblical costumes for the Marys. Mary of Nazareth should hold a small bundle of hay or straw; Mary of Bethany, a few wild or garden flowers; Mary of Jerusalem, a round loaf of bread or a goblet; Mary Magdalene, an alabaster jar.

Group the Four Marys, the first and third seated, the second and fourth standing, around a raised wooden cross containing a large lighted candle in the center and four lighted candles in the arms, head, and foot. Cover stools for the seated Marys with soft drapery. The chancel makes a suitable setting. If a stage and curtain are used, the curtain may be opened and closed slowly during the "Light of the World" solo. The words of the Leader may be adapted to several kinds of service: Easter, Christmas, Mother's Day, Installation of new officers, and so on. For an Installation Service, it is effective to have the Marys light from the Cross a candle for each of the new officers. This service has been used many times at mother-daughter affairs, since Mary of Nazareth and Mary of Jerusalem may be older women, while Mary of Bethany and Mary Magdalene may be quite young. If no soloist is available, the service is effective with the group singing the hymns. Music and words may be found in most hymnals.

OPENING HYMN: *O FOR A THOUSAND TONGUES TO SING*
SOLOIST: *The whole world was lost in the darkness of sin!*
> *The Light of the World is Jesus!*
> *Like sunshine at noonday His glory shone in!*
> *The Light of the World is Jesus!*
> *Come to the Light! 'Tis shining for Thee!*
> *Softly that light has dawned upon me!*
> *Once I was blind, but now I can see*
> *The Light of the World is Jesus!*

Ever at the center of our Christian faith is a radiant figure, Jesus, the Light of the World. The circle of Christian fellowship is wide, indeed, encircling the whole earth, many cultures, many peoples, yet always at its center is Jesus, Author and Finisher of our faith. For Christianity began not with a code, an ethic, not with a creed, a council, not even with a system of philosophy, but with a person

— a man whose compelling love of others drew them to him and around him until a circle was formed.

Can we leave for a few moments the boundaries of this circle and come again to its center? Can we move from the outer edges — the councils, commissions, committees, the millions, the meetings, the methods — and put heart and mind to remembering Jesus, the historical Jesus, who lived at a point in time and walked this earth? Can we prayerfully and quietly return to the center, the Light of our faith, the Light of the world?

How do we, the women of this age, think of Jesus? Infant holy? Boy in the temple? Preaching to the multitude? With the twelve around him at the Last Supper? Alone on Olivet? Alone on Calvary?

We are women trying in our day and for our time to serve and follow him. Can we picture Jesus tonight as he associated with the women of his time who served and followed him?

The world in which Jesus lived was dark for many, but especially dark for women. Through countless years they had been considered property — property to be bought, sold, used, exchanged, cast aside. Now suddenly, they were persons — persons, valued for their own sake, precious, each one, in the sight of God. Fundamental to us now? A miracle then.

Indeed, Jesus' treatment of the women of his time has been called his greatest miracle. So it must have seemed to them, for they were quick to see and respond to this new evaluation of themselves, this light in their darkness. Women came to that light then, and women come to it still, and by the light of Jesus' teaching have advanced to undreamed-of freedom.

Among many who knew and followed him were four named Mary. We see them tonight around the lighted cross — Mary of Nazareth gave a son, gave him care, gave him loyalty till death. Mary of Bethany took time to learn, to sit at the feet of the Master, listening. Mary of Jerusalem gave her home to be used by Jesus and his friends. Her son wrote the Gospel of Mark. Mary Magdalene ran to tell the news of the Risen Christ. She was the first messenger, the first member of his church. Let us listen as four women named Mary tell us of another age, another time . . .

SOLOIST: *"Silent Night, Holy Night," Verse 1*
(Marys gaze only at lighted cross except when speaking, when they turn slowly during solo and face front.)
FIRST MARY:

I am Mary of Nazareth, mother of Jesus. How humble I felt when the angel of the Lord appeared to me and told me that I had been chosen by God to give his son, the Saviour, to mankind. In thanksgiving I sang:

> *My soul doth magnify the Lord,*
> *And my spirit hath rejoiced in God my Saviour . . .*
> *For he hath regard for the low estate of his handmaiden:*
> *For, behold, from henceforth all generations shall call me blessed."*

Jesus was a beautiful baby! How grieved I felt that he must be born so far from home and that I had only the sweet hay of the manger on which to lay my first-born son! But glory shone round about us that night, and we soon forgot our poor surroundings . . . What a glorious privilege it is to train a child! Jesus was quick and responsive. He loved to listen to the old stories of our people and learn the old songs. Before many years he surpassed me in his understanding. Indeed, he often puzzled the rabbis with his searching questions!

After the death of Joseph, Jesus worked as a carpenter to support the family until the other children were grown. Many times after he left Nazareth and began his ministry, I was afraid. Powerful forces were arrayed against him, and I, like any mother, wanted my son at home, safe, with me. When Jesus was betrayed, my grief was hard to bear. Yet, even in the agony of death, my son remembered me. I can still hear him saying to his beloved disciple, *"John, this is your mother,"* and to me, *"Behold, your son!"*

SOLOIST: *"Take Time to be Holy," Verse 1*
SECOND MARY:

I am Mary of Bethany. Just as Bethlehem holds the honor of being the Master's birthplace, so little Bethany is known as the home of his heart. For it was to my home with Martha, my sister, and Lazarus, my brother, that Jesus liked best to come.

Martha often chided me for spending much time talking to Jesus about the things of the Kingdom and forgetting to do my share of the household chores. But Jesus once told me that God had gifted me with a sense of his presence, and moments of prayer and meditation seem most necessary to me.

Now that Jesus is gone, even Martha wishes she had spent more time listening to him and learning from him, as I did, and less time cleaning the corners and fussing about the meals. Jesus didn't like to see women worried and upset. He wanted us, too, to take time to know God. *(Last six words very slowly.)*

SOLOIST: *"O Happy Home, Where Thou Art Loved the Dearest,"* Verse 1
THIRD MARY:

I am Mary of Jerusalem. My husband left me established in a home, a widow, with one son, John Mark. Our house is large and built so that Jesus and his friends could reach an upper room without entering the house proper. We loved to have Jesus use our home. There was a different *feeling* in the house when he was there. No guest was more welcome or more highly honored.

John Mark and I saw wonderful things happen in our upper room — there the disciples came to prepare the Passover Meal, our Lord's Last Supper; there Magdalene came running with the unbelievable news of the Resurrection; and it was in our upper room that the moving power of the Holy Spirit was first felt.

It is a sacred memory to me now that I gave my home to be used freely by the Master, for thus John Mark came to know and love him, and now serves him. For my son spends his days going about with Peter, telling the wonderful story, and in the evenings he writes — writes all that we know ourselves and all we can learn from others. It is *important*, Mark thinks, to have a *written* record! And as for me — I rejoice to have a son so occupied!

SOLOIST: *"Low in the Grave He Lay, Jesus My Saviour,"* Verse 1
FOURTH MARY:

I am Mary Magdalene. As I hurried along that early morning toward his tomb, the spices in my hands reminded me of that other jar of precious ointment I had broken years before over the feet of Jesus. I remembered how my heart had overflowed with gratitude then and how I had wanted to give him my best gift. For I had been sick, sick in my mind — possessed of the 'seven devils,' as they say — and Jesus had cured me! Forever let me testify to the healing power of the Master.

Like others whom he helped, I followed him then with unwearied devotion, until I, too, stood afar off and watched him die. Then I stood in the garden weeping, my tears falling on the useless spices, for the tomb was empty, and I thought they had stolen away my Lord. Suddenly he spoke to me and called me by name:

"Mary, why weepest thou? Whom seekest thou?" Then he told me to go and tell the others. No one believed at first. Now many have seen and believe, and our fellowship grows daily. But I shall never cease marveling that it was to me, a humble woman, that God's great, glad news was first given.

SOLOIST: *"Come to the light! 'Tis shining for thee!"* Chorus only.
PRAYER FOR ALL MARYS: (A spontaneous prayer should be offered, either this or another. Please do not read the prayer.)

Holy Father, we thank thee for the women of yesterday. We thank thee for their devotion, their sacrifice, their service. We praise and bless thee for all the Marys now gathered around thy shining throne. Truly the coming of thy son brought light into the world for all women and for all mankind.

We pray thy blessing, O God, on the Marys of our day — the mothers, the students, the homemakers, the messengers. Bless those women who, like Mary of Nazareth, bear and rear our precious children. Help them to know how much of thee a child finds in his mother's face and voice and loving hands. Bless those who study, who worship thee with heart and soul and mind — the teachers, the ministers, the missionaries. Bless all those who, like Mary of Bethany, make time in their lives to think and plan and pray.

We ask thy blessing, too, upon the homemakers of the world, the women whose homes, like that of Mary of Jerusalem, radiate the loving spirit, the disciplined body, the healing, serving hands that we feel belonged to thy son Jesus. Call and consecrate young people from such homes to serve thee. Call and consecrate us, that our gifts may be sufficient to care for all in thy service.

Finally, our Father, bless the members of thy spiritual kingdom, those who belong to the living fellowship. We pray that our membership in the church may be more than a scrawl in a dusty book. We pray that it may be the whole scroll of a life lived for thee. Like Mary Magdalene may we who are members also be messengers, joyous and unafraid. Forgive our silence, our inaction, and fill us with the compulsion to go and tell others, to proclaim the Christ, herald his Kingdom on earth. So keep within thy loving care the Marys of this day. Fill our lives with the light at the center of the circle, the Light of the Risen Christ, Mary's son, Jesus, in whose name we pray:

THE LORD'S PRAYER

CLOSING HYMN: *"Lead On, O King Eternal,"* All verses.

BENEDICTION:

> O women of God, kneel, and, silent, pray!
> Then rise and herald the truth this day!
> To women of old and your God, be true!
> *Let Christ live in the world through you!*

Reprinted with permission of the Board of Global Ministries
United Methodist Church

UNLESS —

He held their hands in his
Year after year after year
In hospitals, in homes
In car, in ambulance, beside the road
Held firm their dying hands
And comforted, heard prayers:
'Yea, though I walk through the valley,
Thou art with me . . .'
'Though I take the wings of the morning,
Thou art there . . .'

And no one there —
Not wife, not child,
Not doctor, nurse, friend, priest
Not even stranger —
There
To hold his hand, to hear the prayer . . .

I see
His great kind caring ministering hand
Reaching out in darkness
Groping
Growing cold
Unheld, uncomforted . . .
Unless —
Unless —

O God, was Someone there
To hold his hand, to hear the prayer?

MILKWEED IN FALL

*Will God, Who hides inside each pod
Seeds for a hundred springs,
Neglect to send, when my fall comes,
The necessary wings?*

Clarine Coffin Grenfell is a native of Bangor, Maine, but has spent much of her adult life as educator and writer in New York and Connecticut. She earned her Bachelor of Arts at University of Maine with Phi Beta Kappa honors and her Bachelor of Divinity at Hartford Theological Seminary. She has been at various times the pastor of Methodist churches, chairperson of Departments of English, editor and reading consultant in the Educational Division of *Reader's Digest*. Previous publications include textbooks, religious drama, verse, and non-fiction, selections from which are reprinted in *The Caress and the Hurt*. More recently she has published *Women My Husband Married* and *Roses in December*. Married for many years to the late Reverend Jack Grenfell, Mrs. Grenfell is the mother of a son and two daughters. She is presently director of the Grenfell Reading Center in Orland, Maine. A popular speaker throughout her career, she especially enjoys sharing her prose and verse with live audiences.

Note to fourth printing:

In 1982-84, the two years following the first printing of this book, Mrs. Grenfell has, indeed, shared her prose and verse in live readings to more than twelve thousand people in two hundred different places from Maine to Hawaii. If you would like to order books or invite her to come to your college, library, church, write to Grenfell Reading Center, Orland, Maine 04472.